The House That God Built

The Tabernacle in the Wilderness

By Jeffrey L. Seif
and Zola Levitt

Table of Contents

Introduction

Much has been written on the subject of the wilderness Tabernacle and the Jerusalem Temple. That being the case, one may question why we endeavored to write yet another book on them. Are we just reproducing what has already been written? We don't think so and we trust that you'll agree with us that this approach is quite fresh and very informative.

The Bible is a fascinating Book which promises great rewards to those who search out its treasures. Sadly though, the sacred text has been maligned by men and women who claim to be scholars. Liberal theologians have dissected the Bible and claimed that it's merely the work of ancient poets and philosophers, and not the work of an omniscient God. The Holy Bible is not just a collection of ancient writings; rather, it's the actual Word of God—a tapestry which gives the picture of God's plan throughout the ages.

We want to make that point crystal clear to you, so unlike many of the other works on the Lord's House, we've written this book in normal language, instead of bothering you with abstract theological jargon. We think you will appreciate this approach and hope that you will glean a wealth of information from it.

We have a desire to help folks know the Lord better. The Psalmist said, "Through thy precepts I get understanding" (Psa. 119:104a). We come to know the Lord by becoming acquainted with His Word—the Bible. Anything that helps us to know His Word, helps us to know Him better.

This book delves into the mystery of one of the Scripture's most interesting prophetic pictures. You'll be blessed as you come to better understand the majesty of the message. That's our objective anyway. You be the judge and determine if we've reached it.

Relax, kick up your feet and get ready for a worthwhile

experience. You are going to enjoy this book and you'll benefit from it as well.

Jeffrey Seif   Zola Levitt

I

"That I Might Dwell Among My People"

When was the last time someone told you how nice you looked? We often hear statements like, "Oh, what a lovely outfit you're wearing" or "My, what a handsome suit you've got on!" Yes, we Americans certainly like to get dressed up. Madison Avenue is well aware of this and they're constantly throwing a variety of new trends our way, manipulating us to throw billions of our hard earned dollars into the fashion industry. Why do we do it? It's all part of our desire to make a statement to the world about who we are.

A man who frequently wears three-piece suits is likely telling the world that he is on the more conservative side of things, while on the other hand, a young lady who opts for disco outfits and dyes her hair purple is saying that she leans toward the liberal side of the spectrum.

There are myriad examples, but the point is obvious; people are interested in speaking to the world through the images they project. A picture is worth a thousand words and we are all walking pictures. It's all about making a statement to others about ourselves.

It isn't just our clothes. We speak to the world very clearly through the type of homes we live in. There we show our tastes, social status, etc. Most of us spend our money on what we like to call "creature comforts". This isn't just a matter of comfort; it often involves style. But it isn't only style either; rather, it's a statement.

We mortals aren't the only ones who make a statement through the kinds of homes we live in. God did this very thing some 3,500 years ago. He built a house, too. His dwelling had a fenced-in yard, a special doorway, a room that only selected guests could enter, a room for preparing food, etc. He Himself designed all the furniture; all the fabrics were chosen by Him, as were all the colors. God left nothing to the imagination of His construction foreman, Moses, commanding, "According to all that I shew thee, after the pattern of the tabernacle, and the pattern of all the instruments thereof, even so shall ye make it" (Exod. 25:9).

Did you ever see the TV commercial for a magazine that takes us into the homes of the world's wealthiest people? The effect is similar to the successful television show called "The Lifestyles of the Rich and Famous". That sort of thing seems to interest many of us. Everyone is into making a statement and we're interested in seeing what the folks with really big resources can state about themselves.

Our God owns the "cattle on a thousand hills" (Psa. 50:10). But never mind just livestock, for David tells us, "The earth is the Lord's, and the fulness thereof; the world, and they that dwell therein" (Psa. 24:1). God is overwhelmingly famous; yet, it seems that few are interested in His house!

Sadly, the house of the Lord has even escaped the interest of many Christians. "Oh, that's the Old Testament...," some will say. Even if it were just the Old Testament, the God of the Old Testament is the same God of the New one. After all, the Lord said that He is, "The same yesterday, and today, and forever" (Heb. 13:8). Since the God of the Apostle Paul is the same one that Moses encountered, we can assume that we can learn of Him through His dealings with all men throughout all ages.

That being the case, we shall journey back to the dawn of recorded history. Three thousand and five hundred years ago, God, who never changes, manifested Himself to this rather unique fellow named Moses. There were those who would have criticized Him for His choice. After all, there were plenty of powerful people to choose from.

But God overlooked all the rich and famous of the time and placed His favor upon a fugitive desert shepherd whose only employment was the flock of sheep he tended for his father-in-law in the land of Midian.

He didn't seem a very likely candidate, but nonetheless Moses became the Lord's man of the hour! God sent His ambassador back to the land of his birth to confront the world's most powerful dictator, the mighty Pharaoh of Egypt. "Let my people go" (Exod. 5:1) was the message, but Pharaoh wasn't impressed. Finally, following a series of devastating plagues, the children of Israel were loosed from the oppressive bond which held them in slavery for over four hundred years. And so, back to the desert goes Moses, only this time his flock consists of some two million former slaves.

Needless to say, it was a job of emancipation well done!

It was a long and arduous trip to Mount Sinai. With Israel encamped at the base of the mountain, Moses ascended the heights in order to get instructions about his next move.

The Lord didn't just give Moses a few commandments and then send him on his way. Along with the decalogue, Moses was given the complete plans for a prodigious and sumptuous Tabernacle, which he was to construct immediately. It was to be a mysterious worship facility, a manor with hidden meanings whose secrets would keep theologians at their investigative work for thousands of years to come.

God wanted a very special house! In Jewish theology it's known as the *Mishkan* (pronounced mish-kahn) and in our language, Tabernacle. Today in Israel many devout Jewish people are zealous to rebuild the ancient worship center that captivated the hearts of the forefathers ever since the days of antiquity. Why is it so important to them? What's all the fuss?

Granted, it sounds incredible; yet, the fact of the matter

is that the Temple was, and again will be, God's earthly dwelling place! It's the place He selected to live among His people. There are over fifty whole chapters in the Bible that give clues to the enigmas hidden in the blueprints of the Tabernacle. Fifty chapters is no small number. It must be quite important. Here is a small sampling of biblical books with their number of Tabernacle chapters: thirteen chapters in Exodus, eighteen chapters in Leviticus, thirteen chapters in Numbers and two chapters in Deuteronomy. There are plenty more, but why belabor the point? You'll see as you progress through this book that there is a great deal to be said about Old Testament worship and the Tabernacle that was the center of it.

There's a lot invested in the subject of God's house, but that shouldn't surprise us. After all, don't we place a lot of emphasis on how we present ourselves to the world? Consider what you spend on your house, cars, clothes, make-up, jewelry, etc. You'll be amazed to learn how much you invest in your image. This isn't just bare necessities and the like; rather, it's image making. We do it because we realize how important it is to communicate through the images we project. We are saying something.

Do you remember the old saying, "Appearances can be deceiving?" This may well be true in the case of us mortals, but not so with the appearance that God projects. Let's face it, it's rather difficult for an invisible God to impress us with a visual image. We mortals have it a lot easier in that regard. But you can learn a lot about a person by the kind of home they live in, can't you?

God would speak with Moses face to face (Deut. 34:10). The rest of the children of Israel weren't so fortunate, but God wanted to have a relationship with them as well. He wanted them to know Him too. So what did the Lord do? He built a house and stuck it right in the middle of their neighborhood!

God Almighty is making a statement and the potency of

that statement has not diminished over the millenia. It's a mystery that had meaning to the Israelites of bygone days, has meaning for the Church today and will have even more meaning to those who live during the Kingdom era.

You will be blessed as you roll up your sleeves and probe the mystery of the house that God built. Over the river and through the Word to God the Father's House we go!

II

"The Neighbors"

> And the Lord spake unto Moses, saying, Speak unto the children of Israel, that they bring me an offering; of every man that giveth it willingly with his heart ye shall take my offering. And this is the offering which ye shall take of them; gold, and silver, and brass, and blue and purple, and scarlet and fine linen, and goats' hair, and rams' skins dyed red, and badgers' skins, and shittim wood, oil for the light, spices for anointing oil, and for sweet incense, onyx stones, and stones to be set in the ephod, and in the breastplate. *And let them make me a sanctuary; that I may dwell among them* (Exod. 25:1-8).

Do you want God to dwell in your neighborhood? If so, why don't you talk to your pastor and see if you can encourage him to build a Tabernacle? Erect it right next to the church. Can you imagine the kind of growth your church will experience with God Almighty living right next door? All the instructions are right in the Bible (Exod. 25:1 - 27:21). Just build it the way God said to. You could even be the High Priest!

Please forget it! The truth of the matter is that that particular verse isn't talking to the Church. God said, "Let them make me a sanctuary; that I may dwell among *them*" (Exod. 25:8). Question: Who is "them" in the text? Granted it sounds like a silly question, but unlike the previous paragraph, it isn't meant to be silly.

Perhaps you're thinking, "But it's Israel of course!" Believe us, the question isn't frivolous, and the answer

"Israel" isn't sufficient! If you were asked, "*What* were they?" The answer, "Israelites," would suffice. But we asked "*Who* were they?" and the tag "Israelites" doesn't tell us about the peculiar character of the recipients of this wilderness Tabernacle.

Before examining what it was that God had given, let's first develop an understanding of who it was that the Lord gave the Tabernacle to.

Remember, while Moses was up on Mount Sinai receiving the law, many of the "Chosen People" at the base of the mountain were having a licentious orgy. A large number had forsaken God altogether and constructed a golden calf! Moses was up there fellowshipping with the Father, but many of the other children of Israel were in an entirely different frame of mind (see Exod. 32:1-6).

With that event as the backdrop, God imparts the following words to Moses:

> Go, get thee down (from the mountain); for thy people, which thou broughtest out of the land of Egypt, have corrupted themselves: they have turned aside quickly out of the way which I commanded them: they have made them a molten calf, and have worshipped it, and have sacrificed thereunto, and said, These be thy gods, O Israel, which have brought thee up out of the land of Egypt (Exod. 32:7,8).

It is interesting to note that the Lord usually calls Israel "My people", but in this case, He says to Moses, "Get thee down; for *thy* people, which *thou* broughtest out of the land of Egypt...."

Did you ever get angry with your children? It's interesting how when we brag about our kids we always speak of them as "our" children, or as "my" child, but when we are angry with them, we'll yell at our spouse saying, "Now you go tell *your* son...." When we're mad at them, they usually belong to someone else!

Furthermore, Moses wasn't really the one who brought them out of the land of Egypt. He didn't even want to go back for them in the first place. When God first approached Moses with the notion, Moses responded with something like, "You've got the wrong man." Moses had nothing but objections about the whole idea in the first place. God overcame all his objections and then sent Moses off to do His bidding.

An analysis of the Lord's attitude is interesting, but what we really need to keep in mind is that there was a real crisis. Needless to say, Israel wasn't in the best of spiritual conditions at the time. The Jewish people who walked through the Red Sea were hardly a nation of altar boys. Many were rebellious all the way from the sea to the mountain. Every step of the journey was marked with complaining (see Exod. 15:22 - 18:27). Finally, when Moses was gone for a few days (atop Sinai), they didn't just complain against God; rather, many went and invented a brand new god!

Now that we have established that these people were sinners just like the rest of us, let's examine other aspects of their personality.

For over four hundred years the Jewish people had suffered beneath the horrendous yoke of Egyptian bondage. Granted, it wasn't the eternal torment spoken of elsewhere in Scripture (hell), but it surely must have seemed like eternity to them.

They were born as slaves and they died as slaves. Whatever the God of Abraham, Isaac and Jacob stood for didn't seem to matter. He had long since vanished from their thinking. They didn't have hope and they didn't have a Bible to comfort themselves with. All they could do was dry their tears and try to survive.

Then Moses comes bursting into their camp and suddenly they're out in the middle of a desert! There they were following a fairly unknown personality who was following a relatively unknown God. They were in an unknown desert enroute to an unknown land. Well, it was time to get some understanding!

Moses finally came down from that mountain, and he came with more than just a list of rules for them. Of course there were the Ten Commandments, but along with them came a whole new system of worship that would revolve around a house he was instructed to build.

At this juncture it's important to come to grips with a fact that is often overlooked; just about all of the children of Israel couldn't read. They were illiterate. These were the children of slaves. Should we assume that Pharaoh sent them to college? These were slaves who were "educated" if they knew how to spell their names. Of course there were exceptions, but by and large, what amount of knowledge can one expect from two million people who have just come through such a terrible ordeal?

That being the case, what would be the value of just giving them a written law? They wouldn't have been able to read it. And even if they could, how would you produce enough copies to circulate among them? The printing press was thousands of years down the road, after all.

Of course, God did instruct Moses and, under inspiration, he both wrote down the law and communicated it to the elders. But, at this juncture, the primary means of teaching the Israelites was through what they could *see*!

Most couldn't read or write, but they all could see the world around them. Their minds weren't yet fully developed but their eyes were, and they all could behold this special Tabernacle in their midst. They would sit at the door of their tents and watch the smoke of the various offerings ascend toward heaven.

No doubt they were intrigued as they observed the officiating priesthood busily attending to the services of this newly erected sanctuary. They could smell the perfumed incense as it ascended upward to this one God. No, these people couldn't yet read the law, but don't pity them; they could *see it*!

The God of their fathers had moved into the neighborhood! He was making a statement, and His picture was literally worth 10,000 words!

It was time to learn about monotheism. These were awesome and significant days for the Hebrew people.

The new worship center needed to be financed. Where did the money come from? That question is answered when we turn our attention to their last moments in Egypt. It's interesting the way the King James Version Bible puts it:

> And the children of Israel did according to the word of Moses; and they *borrowed* of the Egyptians jewels of silver, and jewels of gold, and raiment. And the Lord gave the people favour in the sight of the Egyptians, so that they *lent* unto them such things as they required...(Exod. 12:35,36).

What does it mean that the Egyptians "lent" the Jews whatever they needed for their journey, and that the Hebrews "borrowed" jewels and the like from the Egyptians? It sounds almost comical. "Excuse me, Mr. Overseer. We're going on a long journey. We don't have any plans to ever return, but we'd like to know if we can *borrow* your fine jewels. When we get to our Promised Land, the first thing we will do will be to send you a money order."

A closer examination of the language says that the Jewish people *took* whatever they wanted from the Egyptians, period! The Egyptians were completely disoriented as a result of the plagues that befell them. Their attitude was, "Take what you want, but just get out of here!" The Hebrews took off with all the gold they could carry and when their pockets were full, the donkeys and camels were loaded up! Where did they get all the livestock? They took a lot of that, too!

Let's face it, the Israelites were working there for a very long time. Four hundred-plus years is a long time to go without pay. Yes, the Jewish people took what they could as back wages, or reparations, with God's blessing.

Three months later, at the foot of Mount Sinai, Israel gets the word that it's time to build a house for the Lord. They were wealthy with goods at the time. It is interesting to note how they were to give of their newly acquired sustenance:

> And the Lord spake unto Moses, saying, Speak unto the children of Israel, that they bring me an offering: *of every man that giveth it willingly from his heart* ye shall take my offering (Exod. 25:1,2).

God wants people to give from their hearts. That is how the Church is built, too. It is sad how many rely on slick commercial approaches to raise funds to build church buildings and the like. The Lord's people ought to give from the heart. If a meeting hall is built using such techniques, that's what you'll have when it's finished--just a meeting hall. It may look like a church and may even sound like one, but the real thing exists only when there are folks who care about the Lord and want to give from their hearts for the work of the ministry. That is how the first house was built and how all the following ones must be built.

Returning to the text itself now, we see that it was their gold that went into the making of the Tabernacle, and it was their sacrifices that were burnt there in order to appease a God who only recently slew thousands of their friends and brethren for putting their gold into the making of a golden calf.

They learned quickly that this was indeed a jealous God (Exod. 20:5). Again we stress: these were significant days for Israel, and for all the godly to follow throughout the ages.

When we are hungry, we go out and buy some food. Well, there weren't many stores out there in the wilderness. The K-Marts were few and far between, and the Pizza Inns hadn't even been invented yet! Can you imagine that? It is easy to understand how this newly born nation must have had a real appreciation for healthy livestock. You'll never guess what the God of Israel wanted from them next! He demanded that the best of their livestock be burnt in His kitchen! It would go up in smoke and the people would just stand by and watch. The nourishment went into God's nostrils instead of their stomachs. Wouldn't this have a profound effect on you if you were there?

They must have wondered about it. Why does He want it? Why? Why? Why? Perhaps they said, "If God loves smoke in the atmosphere, couldn't He just wait until the 20th century? By that time the air will be full of smoke!

It wasn't just that they would sacrifice their best livestock; rather, it was the method by which they'd do it. Adult Israelites would no doubt put on their Sunday best (actually Saturday best) when it was time for them to visit the house of the Lord. They'd dress up and take the best animal that they had and off they'd go to "church".

Once inside the Tabernacle courtyard, they'd lay both hands on the innocent animal, recite a prayer hoping that God would receive this offering in payment of their sins, and then cut the throat themselves, ending the life of this helpless creature. After draining the blood, the priest would then take the carcass and burn it on the altar, ending up with just a charred corpse.

It wasn't pretty, and it wasn't meant to be. Sin isn't pretty.

They would then return home with the memory of that experience still fresh on their minds. The bloodstains would be on their hands, and on their garments as well. On top of that, the stench would remain in their hair and on their clothes.

Just think of what they had to go through. No doubt they did! We began this book by saying that God was making a statement. Question: what kind of messages came through in all of this? Answers:

1. There really is only one God. He is real and is part of our history. We owe our freedom to Him.

2. God is a jealous God! He will punish those who worship other so-called gods.

3. He wants us to give willingly from our hearts.

4. He is a righteous God.

5. There are penalties for sin. Sin brings death, and life must be taken in atonement for sins. In their case, it was an innocent animal that died.

6. There is something special about the blood.

It certainly is likely that they would have gleaned other insights as well from the God who dwelt in their neighborhood. These which we listed should serve to demonstrate the point presented at the outset, namely that God used the Tabernacle to communicate to His people and to make a statement about Himself. We hope you are getting the point.

The primary message of the Tabernacle sounded something like this:

> "I am the Lord thy God. I live right in the center of your neighborhood. Do you see My house there in the middle of the camp? I reside there. You must deal with Me. If you reject Me, you'll die! If you obey Me, you'll live!
>
> That's My house there in the middle of the camp. You'll need to visit Me constantly. You must come when you have sin. Come when you need to, and believe Me, you'll need to.
>
> And when you come, do remember a very important fact. Do not, I repeat, do not come with empty hands! I'll need some of that real good livestock of yours. Kill it and give it to Me! If you don't, I'll kill you. I am the Lord thy God and I live right next door!
>
> Can you smell the stench of the thousands of slain animals there in My courtyard? Can you see the smoke--that large pillar of smoke? It doesn't smell so good, does it?
>
> Sometimes the wind will blow it one direction and sometimes in another direction. One day the whole of it will blow your way, and on another day it'll blow towards somebody else's tent. It's a terrible smell, isn't it?
>
> That's My house but it isn't My smell. If you hate the odor, that's not My problem, it's yours. Those are your sins you are smelling, not Mine!

> Do you get the point? I'm patient. If you don't get it today, then perhaps you'll get it tomorrow. I'm not planning any vacations. I'll be around for quite a while.
>
> That's My house over there in the middle of your camp. I live right next door and I'm making a statement.
>
> Do you get the message?

The point of this chapter, up until now, has been twofold: First, to increase your understanding of the Israelite people to whom the law was given, and secondly, to enable you to see the Tabernacle from their vantage point. Having stimulated your awareness of the bloody nature of the law given to Moses, it behooves us to spend a few moments to address what critics have called "the slaughterhouse religion" of the Old Testament. Let's tell it like it is: there's a lot of blood and guts in all of this. Many millions of animals have gone up in smoke to appease the God of Abraham. For that reason, some philosophical social scientists want nothing to do with our blood-drenched Bible.

"How could a loving God do it?" they ask. They miss the point. If they really want to throw stones, there's an even better target to aim at. Why not contend by asking, "How could a loving father murder his only son?" That's exactly what God did in the New Testament and that is exactly what He was teaching in the Old Testament!

We don't find the concept of sacrifice in the creation plan of Genesis. Sacrifice came into the picture only after sin had made its ignoble entrance into the drama. It was only after the "fall" that a means for expiation became necessary.

Blood sacrifice is a scarlet thread woven throughout the pages of the Bible, from Genesis to Revelation. It's a tapestry that makes a signpost which points directly to the Messiah, Jesus Christ.

The Apostle Peter, in I Peter 1:10-12 explains:

> ...the prophets...testified beforehand the sufferings of Christ, and the glory that should follow. Unto whom it was revealed, that not unto themselves, but unto us they did minister the things, which are now reported to you....

Those who mock the blood of Moses mock the cross of Christ! Granted, it's an ugly business, but it's our sin that brought it about. This is the basic message and it appeared as soon as the time was ripe for the documenting of Holy Writ.

The ministry of Moses marked the advent of a very important era. Moses was a writer! The record of documented revelation begins with this man of God. After him came the priests, prophets and kings, who themselves were also inspired to preserve what God was saying in written form. The collection of their writings is found in the book commonly called the Old Testament.

Four hundred years pass after the Old Testament is completed and an angel pays a visit to the Virgin Mary, thus marking the dawn of the New Testament. The drama continues as inspired men document the accounts of Christ's life in detailed biographies. Epistles also surfaced as it was necessary to provide the fledgling Church with a handbook for the instruction and nurturing of the believers.

It all began one-and-a-half thousand years before the Messiah with the introduction of those written tablets containing the Ten Commandments. Moses received the writing assignment and became God's hand and pen, as the Lord put it all in permanent form.

It is very important to understand that God didn't only

tell Moses to write a book; in addition He told him to build a building. The Tabernacle was built immediately; right at the advent of God's recorded revelation.

God gave Israel both a law and a house, together. The one came with the other; in fact, you really can't separate the two. God's word and God's house mean much less without each other. Without the Tabernacle you simply could not follow the law, and without the law you simply could not make sense out of the Tabernacle. This exchange is the very essence of the Law of Moses.

The Law of Moses is the basis of the Old Testament. It is as essential to the Old Testament as the heart is to the human body. The law is the sun and the prophets, Jeremiah, Daniel, Ezekiel, etc., are the planets that revolve around that sun.

The New Testament is the continuing story of the Old Testament. It isn't a "new" story; rather, it's the fulfillment of the "old" one. The New Testament records the plant that sprouted forth from the flower bed of the Old Testament. The Old Testament is the New Testament concealed and the New Testament is the Old Testament revealed. The Old is the arm and the New is the hand that extends from it, and together they tell the story of a heavenly Father reaching out to wayward children, calling them home to the One from whom they have strayed (I Peter 2:25).

Now let's trace this relationship backwards. The New Testament is built upon the Old Testament and the Old Testament is built upon the Law of Moses. That being the case, the New Testament has the Law of Moses as its very foundation. Listen to what the King says on this very point:

> For had ye believed Moses, ye would have believed me: for he wrote of me. But if ye believe not his writings, how shall ye believe my words? (John 5:46, 47)

Jesus is saying that if they couldn't come to terms with the writings of Moses, they wouldn't be able to come to terms with Him.

We need to understand Moses in order to fully appreciate Jesus. In order to fully grasp the essence of Moses one needs to understand the Tabernacle, because without the Tabernacle there really is no way to follow the teachings of Moses. The one is the real-life example of the other. The Tabernacle was God's audio-visual aid to demonstrate the Law of Moses, which itself is the very core of the Gospel message. It's Jesus' backbone, the very foundation upon which the New Testament rests.

It all began when God gave Moses those awesome commandments and sent him down the mountain to build a house.

Moses was up there on that mountain for quite a while (Exod. 24:18). Needless to say, he would likely have been a little anxious to come down. Well, he wasn't the only one interested in coming down for *God wanted to come down, too*!

After all, it wasn't Moses who brought Israel to God; rather, it was God who brought Israel to Himself (Jer. 31:32). The Lord wanted to be with His Chosen People!

God wanted to get down from that mountain and dwell among His people. He has a special feeling for these people. Listen to what the Lord says in Jeremiah 31:3:

> ...Yea, I have loved thee with an *everlasting* love: therefore with lovingkindness have I drawn thee.

The Tabernacle was God's apartment on earth! It wasn't just that the Lord wanted to have a house in their neighborhood, but that He wanted all Israel to be able to come and fellowship with Him often.

Moses was a totally unique individual. In fact, God called Moses His "friend" (Exod. 33:11). Moses could commune with the Father directly, but the rest, all two million Israelites, weren't quite as fortunate. Let's face it, men like Moses weren't exactly growing on trees. That fruit was one-of-a-kind. He was the leader but God loved the rest as well. So, the house of God was constructed as a means by which all men and women could have a relationship with the God of Abraham, Isaac and Jacob. God Almighty wanted their fellowship as well.

We don't want to paint the picture of a lonely God. In our case, we need Him: in His case, He wants us! If someone wants to reject Him that's his business, but it's not God who is the real loser. We're not doing God any favors by being "religious". It isn't He that needs the help. As Jeremiah pointed out:

> O Lord, I know that the way of man is not in himself: it is not in man that walketh to direct his steps (Jer. 10:23).

We're the ones who need direction in life. The Lord needs us about as much as we need our children's help in driving our cars.

Our heavenly Father isn't interested in simply dwelling on high, far removed from the human condition. Of course, His majesty is all important; yet, He willingly set it aside in order to reach a dying world. This concept is made manifest in His sending Jesus!

> ...Jesus...made Himself of no reputation, and took upon Him the form of a servant, and was made in the likeness of men... (Paul, in Phil. 2:7).

In all of this Jesus was simply following the Father's example. Listen to Messiah's own words, as recorded in the Gospel of John:

> ...Verily, verily, I say unto you (notice the emphasis), The Son can do nothing of himself, but what he seeth the Father do: for what things soever he doeth, these also doeth the Son likewise (John 5:19).

"For God so loved the world, that He gave His only begotten Son..." (John 3:16). Jesus took on a body and came to pay us a visit. Likewise, in the Old Testament God, who desired to come down for a visit, took on a Temple.

The wilderness Tabernacle is the John 3:16 of the Old Testament.

Jesus is the "door" (John 10:9) and the Levitical law is the key which opens that door, for through it we may perceive the Gospel in all its glory. The only way to fully understand Jesus is to understand Moses, and the only way to understand Moses (even remotely) is to understand the Tabernacle. And finally, the only way to understand the Tabernacle is to become acquainted in detail with what the Scriptures say concerning it.

III

"The House That God Built"

For many, the laws of Moses are like the multiple laws of the Internal Revenue Service. Do you understand the intricate inner workings of our tax system? Most people treat the law of Moses just like the I. R. S. code: we'll try to respect it, but we have given up trying to understand it.

We are going to explain a lot of it for you, but at this juncture we think it's a good idea for you to reacquaint yourself with the headquarters of this Old Testament "Internal Revenue System". The instructions for the construction of the Tabernacle begin in Exodus 25 and conclude in Exodus 27. There is no substitute for reading the original--God's Word--and we urge you to take up your Bible now and do that.

Don't allow yourself to get flustered by what seems to be a maze of pointless details. It's not a maze and the details certainly aren't pointless. Putting all of the scriptural details together in a form that can be easily digested isn't as hard as it may seem. Granted, we are at a disadvantage, but the task isn't impossible.

The Jews in Bible days at least had something to look at. The Tabernacle was there. In that, we are not so fortunate. We've provided a picture that should help to explain the thousand words that you've just read. It's a bird's eye view of the worship facility being described in the previous quotations. Take a moment to become acquainted with it.

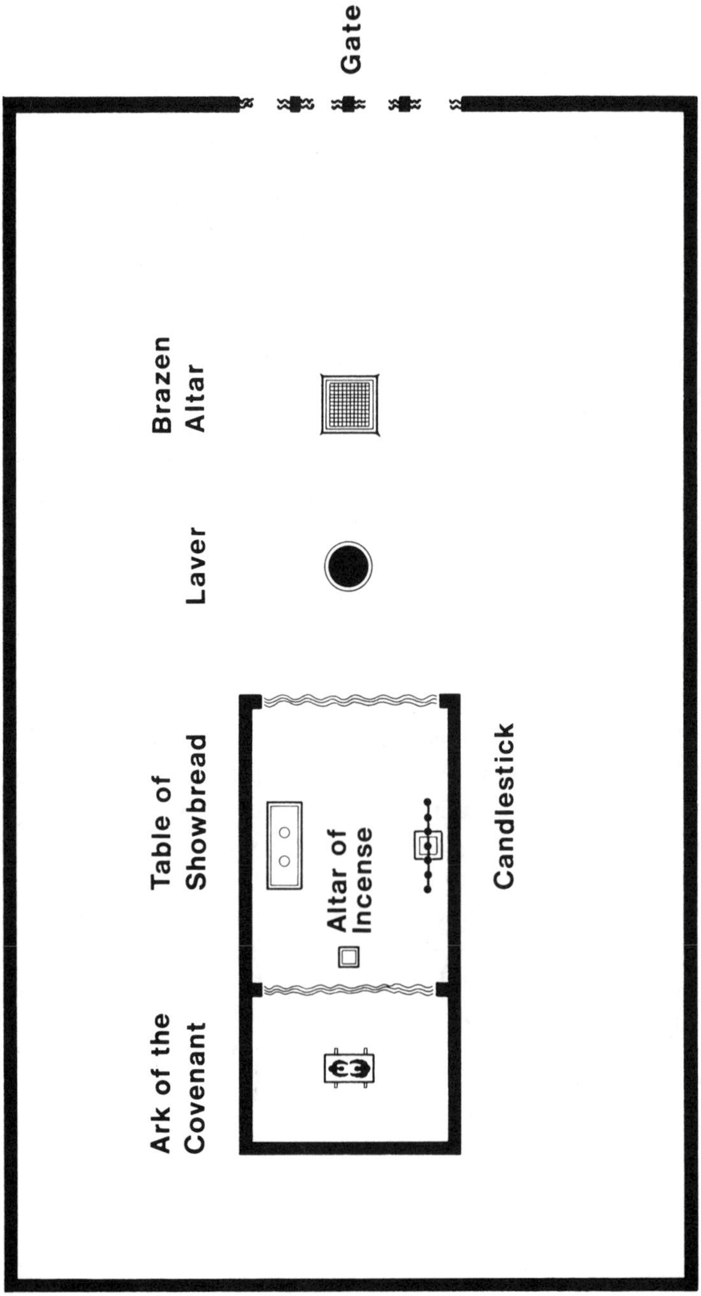
Gate
Brazen Altar
Laver
Table of Showbread
Altar of Incense
Candlestick
Ark of the Covenant

Now here are some basic observations that explain some important points of interest:

1. Notice that the entrance is on the east side of the worship complex. There was only *one way* into God's presence, just as there still is only one way--Messiah. Everyone coming to worship would enter there. They would go as far as the brazen altar. There they would slaughter their sacrifice by cutting it's throat. The carcass would then be handed over to the priest, who in turn would offer the sacrifice on behalf of the party needing expiation.

2. The rectangle which encompasses the entire complex represents the special fence which surrounded the entire area. Inside was the courtyard and outside were the people. It wasn't that God needed to be kept inside. On the contrary, it was the people who needed to be kept out. People weren't to approach God from a hundred directions. Today, there are a myriad of religions, each with their own special twist. They aren't going to get anywhere near the God of Israel.

3. Inside the large rectangle is a smaller one which represents the actual sanctuary, but more on that in a moment.

4. **The Brazen Altar** - This was the place for sacrifice, the Golgotha (Matt. 27:33; Mark 15:22; John 19:17) of the Old Testament. Only priests could approach the Lord beyond this altar. The common man and woman could go no further.

5. **The Laver** - This was the place for washing. One had to cleanse himself prior to entering God's presence to minister in the sanctuary. This is where the priests would wash. It's crucial to remember that the priest would first make an offering for his own sins and then, and **only** then, would he wash in preparation for entry into his priestly service in God's sanctuary: first came the altar and then came the water. We'll be talking more about this very critical point.

6. **The Table of Shewbread** - Twelve pieces of unleavened bread were displayed on this table. Why? Wait and see! (Hint: sustenance).

7. **The Candlestick (or Menorah)** - There always needed to be a perpetual light burning in the Holy Place. As we delve into this mystery your understanding of Jesus will no doubt be illuminated.

8. **The Incense Altar** - A prescribed incense was burnt at this altar. It had to be authentic. In particular, embers had to be taken from the brazen altar and used for this ritual. Short cuts were not tolerated. Aaron, the first High Priest, suffered the loss of two sons who tried to save time with their own brand of incense (see Num. 26:60,61).

9. **The Ark of the Covenant** - Having examined the furniture that was placed inside the Holy Place, we'll now proceed through the Veil and into the Holy of Holies, where the Ark was kept. The Ark was a hollow chest that

housed three sacred artifacts: First, the tablets of the Ten Commandments; second, Aaron's rod, which budded (see Heb. 9:4 and Num. 17:8-10); third and lastly, a bowl of wilderness food (manna). On top of the Ark were figurines of two angelic beings, whose outstretched wings would act as a sort of canopy over the Ark. Between these two beings was the "Mercy Seat". This was the Lord's throne, the very place where He would dwell.

Before moving on, let's briefly recap what we've just learned:

BRAZEN ALTAR = Sacrifice for sins

LAVER = Washing, Ritual Purification

TABLE OF SHEWBREAD = Life, Sustenance

CANDLESTICK = Light

INCENSE ALTAR = Prayer

ARK = God's dwelling

There exists a remarkable parallel between the Gospel of John and the wilderness Tabernacle. In fact, it has been suggested that John's Gospel is simply a walk through the Tabernacle. There is much to be said for that statement. Pay careful attention to the following and you'll find out why.

John begins his Gospel by calling attention to Jesus as the Lamb of God with the exclamation of the Baptist, "Behold the Lamb of God which taketh away the sin of the world" (John 1:29). Some of God's best lambs shared the same destiny; they were doomed to breathe their last breath at the brazen altar. Let us remember that the Tabernacle was a great place for men and women, but it was a terrible place for sheep! They were destined to die there. Their life instead of the sinner's, in a symbolic taking away of the sins of those who brought them for sacrifice. The act of sacrifice is step one in the Tabernacle and it's no accident that John likewise goes right to it.

The second stop was the place for washing - the Laver. John quickly takes us there..."Verily, verily, I say unto thee, Except a man be born of *water* and of the Spirit, he cannot enter into the kingdom of God" (John 3:5). From there John takes us to the Baptist; "...and John also was baptizing...because there was much water in the place" (John 3:23). In chapter four we have the story of the woman at the well (John 4:6ff), and in chapter five Jesus pays a visit to the pool at Bethesda (John 5:2-9).

The Gospel begins with an exclamation about the Lamb of God who will take away the sins of the world (John 1:29). From there he takes us to the water of regeneration--baptism (John 3:5); to the "living water" (John 4:10), and then to the healing waters of the pool at Bethesda (John 5:2,3).

The next piece of furniture that one comes to in the Tabernacle is the Table of Shewbread. Let's see what happens next in the Gospel of John.

In chapter six, Jesus goes into a rather lengthy discourse on how He is the "bread of life" (John 6:48ff). He goes on to explain in detail, saying:

> I am the bread of life...I am the living bread which came down out of heaven: if any man (or woman) eat of this bread, he shall live forever... (John 6:48-51).

After a stop at the Table of Shewbread, the priest then

turns his attention to the Menorah in the Tabernacle. It's no accident that our next stop on our journey through takes us to a discourse wherein our Lord is saying the following:

> ...I am the light of the world: he that followeth me shall not walk in darkness but shall have the light of life (John 8:12).

In the following chapter, what does the Messiah do? He goes on to heal a blind man; in other words, He gives light to the blind (John 9:1-11). It's all about light, isn't it?

The following chapters of the Gospel of John (10-16) take us to the end of His earthly ministry. Therein the Lord gives instructions about the Holy Spirit, abiding in Him, peace, overcoming problems, etc. It all relates to prayer.

Finally, in the seventeenth chapter we find the Lord directly in intercessory prayer:

> These words spake Jesus, and lifted up his eyes to heaven, and said, Father, the hour is come; glorify thy Son, that thy Son also may glorify thee:
>
> As thou hast given him power over all flesh, that he should give eternal life to as many as thou hast given him.
>
> And this is life eternal, that they might know thee the only true God, and Jesus Christ, whom thou hast sent.
>
> I have glorified thee on the earth: I have finished the work which thou gavest me to do.

And now, O Father, glorify thou me with thine own self with the glory which I had with thee before the world was.

I have manifested thy name unto the men which thou gavest me out of the world: thine they were, and thou gavest them me; and they have kept thy word.

Now they have known that all things whatsoever thou hast given me are of thee.

For I have given unto them the words which thou gavest me; and they have received them, and have known surely that I came out from thee, and they have believed that thou didst send me.

I pray for them: I pray not for the world, but for them which thou hast given me; for they are thine.

And all mine are thine, and thine are mine; and I am glorified in them.

And now I am no more in the world, but these are in the world, and I come to thee. Holy Father, keep through thine own name those whom thou hast given me, that they may be one, as we are.

While I was with them in the world, I kept them in thy name: those that thou gavest me I have kept, and none of them is lost, but the son of perdition; that the scripture might be fulfilled.

And now come I to thee; and these things I speak in the world, that they might have my joy fulfilled in themselves.

I have given them thy word; and the world hath hated them, because they are not of the world, even as I am not of the world.

I pray not that thou shouldest take them out of the world, but that thou shouldest keep them from the evil.

They are not of the world, even as I am not of the world.

Sanctify them through thy truth: thy word is truth.

As thou hast sent me into the world, even so have I also sent them into the world.

And for their sakes I sanctify myself, that they also might be sanctified through the truth.

Neither pray I for these alone, but for them also which shall believe on me through their word;

That they all may be one; as thou, Father, art in me, and I in thee, that they also may be one in us: that the world may believe that thou hast sent me.

And the glory which thou gavest me I have given them; that they may be one, even as we are one:

> I in them, and thou in me, that they may be made perfect in one; and that the world may know that thou hast sent me, and hast loved them, as thou hast loved me.
>
> Father, I will that they also, whom thou hast given me, be with me where I am; that they may behold my glory, which thou hast given me: for thou lovedst me before the foundation of the world.
>
> O righteous Father, the world hath not known thee: but I have known thee, and these have known that thou hast sent me.
>
> And I have declared unto them thy name, and will declare it: that the love wherewith thou hast loved me may be in them, and I in them (John 17:1-26).

We might say that Jesus was at the Altar of Incense. There our High Priest (Heb. 4:14, 15) is petitioning the Father on our behalf; in other words, He's burning incense for us. For more understanding on prayer and incense, look up the following verses: Psa. 141:2; Rev. 5:8 and Rev. 8:4.

The Gospel narrative proceeds with Messiah's arrest and then the cross. After going into the Holy Place where the Candlestick, Bread and Incense altar were, the High Priest would then go into the Holy of Holies, the place where God dwelt. He would enter with the blood of the sacrifice that was made for the people.

And so it is that the Lord then says to the disciples, "I ascend unto my Father, and your Father; and to my God, and your God" (John 20:17). Our High Priest goes off into God's presence.

It's interesting to note that it is the Veil which separates the Holy Place from the Holy of Holies. Only the High Priest could enter the most sacred place, where God Himself dwelt, while the remaining priests had access to the Holy Place only.

There is much more to be said on all of this spiritual elegance. For now, we will leave the Gospel of John and delve further into the mystery of the Tabernacle.

IV

"According To All That I Show Thee"

Now that we have examined some of the basic interpretations of the wilderness Tabernacle, let's focus our attention on the deeper, more hidden meanings found in the house of the Lord. Our approach here will be very systematic. In other words, we will review what the Bible says and we'll make *observations*. Having done that, we will proceed to make *applications*.

Here's how it will work: we will make applications from our interpretations of our observations! Got it?

Throughout this chapter we will quote voluminous sections of Scripture relating to the physical structure of the Tabernacle. We will comment to some degree on God's meticulous directions and requirements. We would certainly recommend further study in more specialized books to fully appreciate all these intricacies.

> And the Lord spake unto Moses, saying, Speak unto the children of Israel, that they bring me an offering: of every man that giveth it willingly with his heart ye shall take my offering. And this is the offering which ye shall take of them; gold, and silver, and brass, and blue, and purple, and scarlet, and fine linen, and goats' hair, and rams' skins dyed red, and badgers' skins, and shittim wood, Oil for the light, spices for anointing oil, and for sweet incense, Onyx stones, and stones to be set in the ephod, and in the breastplate. And let them make me a sanctuary; that I may dwell among them. According to all that I shew thee, after the pattern of the tabernacle,

> and the pattern of all the instruments thereof, even so shall ye make it (Exod. 25:1-9).

The Lord speaks to Moses in verse two saying that offerings should be given from the heart. We talked about this some already. The point is rather obvious: true sacrificial giving must come from the heart. Jesus told the story about the poor widow who gave two pennies and the rich man who gave a great deal. What is relevant about the story is that the Lord said that the poor woman gave more. The principle there is that it isn't what you give that counts; rather, it's what you have left over after you have given it. In other words, if you have a million dollars in your checking account, it really isn't a very big deal if you write out a check for five thousand dollars. But if you have only one hundred dollars in your account and you give a check for the Lord's work for, let's say, seventy-five dollars or so, then your gift, from God's point of view, is much greater. It is quite obvious that you are giving from your heart. Why? Because the giving really *hurts*!

It was on this very point, and from this very passage in Exodus, that the Orthodox Rabbi from Tarsus (Paul) said the following:

> Every man according as he purposeth in his heart, so let him give; not grudgingly, or of necessity: for God loveth a cheerful giver (II Cor. 9:7).

There are instructions given about metals, colors, fabrics, spices, oils, and precious gems. The people didn't have lots of hundred dollar bills in their pockets. At this point in time the primary means of trade was barter. Goods had an understood value. Each item was worth something in a monetary sense.

God wasn't so much interested in the monetary value of these items. There was a deeper meaning associated with them that went above and beyond dollars and cents. These items are seen elsewhere in the Bible, and certain applications can be made by comparing the various ways in which they are used in the Scriptures.

Precious metals have a very interesting application in the Bible. Gold, the best of them all, is used to convey the idea of deity. Silver corresponds to redemption, while brass corresponds to judgment. Get out your concordance and look up the various passages that use these symbols. You'll have a lot of fun with it!

Colors are quite interesting as well. Take purple for instance. The Tabernacle was draped in a purple robe. The King of Kings wanted this to envelop His sanctuary. Purple is the color of kings. Remember how the soldiers were mocking the Lord saying, "Hail, King of the Jews!" They had put a crown of thorns on His head and a *purple* robe on His back. Well, the King did Himself wear the purple robe, and here in the text we see that the Lord wanted His house to be wrapped in a purple robe as well.

Scarlet (or red) relates so much to sacrifice. It is easy to see that, for this is the color of blood. Blue, on the other hand, directs one's attention not to sin and sacrifice but to heaven. Blue is the color of the sky. It's a placid color and evokes thoughts of tranquility. Of course, one day the Lord will return and take us to be with Him, and there in glory (heaven) we will have peace, and no longer shall there be a tear in our eyes!

A survey of various animal skins used in the Bible yields a wealth of information. Here, for one example, we find the Lord requesting that skins from rams be used. It takes one back to the time when Abraham was about to offer his son Isaac. Just when he was about to slay the lad, a ram was found in the thicket and used in place of the young boy. The skins are dyed red, and herein we find a reminder of the sacrifice for sins. In fact, the ultimate sacrifice was, of course, when God did offer up His only son, who came and shed His blood for our sins. In regard to the usage of skins, it's meaningful to note that just after sin came into the world, the guilty couple (Adam and Eve) put on animal skins (see Gen. 3:21). Now let's face it, to wear a skin you first have to kill the animal who wore that fur before you. Adam and Eve realized they were naked because of sin and animals needed to be slain to cover their nakedness. This is a primitive principle; it appears in the first pages of Holy Writ and remains throughout until the close of the Bible. The skins draped throughout the Tabernacle were a reminder to man why he needed the Tabernacle in the first place. Adam enjoyed fellowship with the Father, but when sin came in, it was necessary to deal with the emergence of this default which drove a wedge in their communion. The skins are a reminder of an old, old story. The Tabernacle was a way that "naked" men and women could be restored to fellowship with the Father.

The stones are interesting to note. Each of the twelve tribes had their own particular gem which represented them, kind of a birth stone. The Lord ultimately gives a white stone (gem) to the saints of Pergamum who overcome (Rev. 2:17). Royalty wears precious gems, not common people. They are more in use today among the ordinary people, but this was not the case in the early days of the Bible. The Lord had precious stones in the Tabernacle showing His royalty. Being that we are a royal priesthood (those who have received the Lord), the stones have a relationship to us (see I Pet. 2:9 for the royal priesthood of believers in Messiah). That's why we can give to the Lord's work from our hearts. Why? Because in glory, we will be adorned with all manner of good things, apparently even precious gems.

> And they shall make an ark of shittim wood: two cubits and a half shall be the length thereof, and a cubit and a half the breadth thereof, and a cubit and a half the height

thereof.

And thou shalt overlay it with pure gold, within and without shalt thou overlay it, and shalt make upon it a crown of gold round about.

And thou shalt cast four rings of gold for it, and put them in the four corners thereof; and two rings shall be in the one side of it, and two rings in the other side of it.

And thou shalt make staves of shittim wood, and overlay them with gold.

And thou shalt put the staves into the rings by the sides of the ark, that the ark may be borne with them.

The staves shall be in the rings of the ark: they shall not be taken from it.

And thou shalt put into the ark the testimony which I shall give thee.

And thou shalt make a mercy seat of pure gold: two cubits and a half shall be the length thereof, and a cubit and a half the breadth thereof.

And thou shalt make two cherubims of gold, of beaten work shalt thou make them, in the two ends of the mercy seat.

And make one cherub on the one end, and the other cherub on the other end: even of the mercy seat shall ye make the cherubims

> on the two ends thereof.
>
> And the cherubims shall stretch forth their wings on high, covering the mercy seat with their wings, and their faces shall look one to another; toward the mercy seat shall the faces of the cherubims be.
>
> And thou shalt put the mercy seat above upon the ark; and in the ark thou shalt put the testimony that I shall give thee.
>
> And there I will meet with thee, and I will commune with thee from above the mercy seat, from between the two cherubims which are upon the ark of the testimony, of all things which I will give thee in commandment unto the children of Israel (Exod. 25:10-22).

One of the first things we notice about the Ark is that it was made of wood overlaid with gold. The Ark was a hollow chest that was used to house certain items of which we have already spoken, and as a base for the throne of God, the Mercy Seat.

Also, there are instructions given for rings to be attached to the Ark and posts to be made that went through the rings. Remember, these Israelites had many more miles to travel before they would actually arrive in the Holy Land. This was a portable worship center, and the particulars of it were made for travel.

The Lord didn't want the priests to touch His Ark! That being the case, means of transporting it without laying hands on it were made as well.

We like to call the Jerusalem Temple God's apartment on earth. Well, this was His mobile home!

Above the Ark were two angelic type beings. Between them was the Mercy Seat, and it was there that God dwelt.

It's interesting to note how the throne is called the "Mercy Seat". Sadly, many religious people don't have any idea what the word means. Here, God is surrounded with all manner of regal pomp. This, of course, is due Him, but the point is that He dwells at a place called Mercy! A king pronounces his judgments from his throne. Many people would no doubt be afraid to approach him in the first place, and when they finally did get a hearing with the king, the fact that the thrones were often decorated with lions and leopards, etc., didn't help to calm their fears. But the throne of God is called the *Mercy Seat*, and it's decorated with gentle angels, not fierce lions.

Furthermore, God's presence dwelt within a fixture made of wood overlaid with gold. It could have just as easily been made of solid gold. Why the wood?

It can be said that gold lasts forever while wood is quite perishable. In the Bible wood is used to describe humanity. Arrogant people are compared to the high and lofty cedars of Lebanon and stubborn immovable people are compared to thick trunked oaks of Bashan (Isa. 2:12-14). Of course, not all are bad. Jesus is compared to a tree ("root out of dry ground" - Isa. 53:2) and the believers are like trees who are to bring forth good fruit. In any event, it is clear that trees represent the human side of things.

Add this to the royal gold (deity) and what do you come up with?: an interesting picture of the Lord Jesus, who Himself was both wood and gold, human and divine. This picture, along with the others that we have mentioned, may be found in the wilderness Tabernacle.

> Thou shalt also make a table of shittim wood: two cubits shall be the length thereof, and a cubit the breadth thereof, and a cubit and a half the height thereof.
>
> And thou shalt overlay it with pure gold, and make thereto a crown of gold round

> about.
>
> And thou shalt make unto it a border of an hand breadth round about, and thou shalt make a golden crown to the border thereof round about.
>
> And thou shalt make for it four rings of gold, and put the rings in the four corners that are on the four feet thereof.
>
> Over against the border shall the rings be for places of the staves to bear the table.
>
> And thou shalt make the staves of shittim wood, and overlay them with gold, that the table may be borne with them.
>
> And thou shalt make the dishes thereof, and spoons thereof, and covers thereof, and bowls thereof, to cover withal: of pure gold shalt thou make them.
>
> And thou shalt set upon the table shewbread before me always (Exod. 25: 23-30).

The Table of Shewbread is a favorite of ours. First of all, it's so easy to understand. Why? Because the Lord had so much to say about bread. Secondly, it's so essential to life both physically and spiritually.

Twelve pieces of flat bread were arranged on this table (see Lev. 24:6). This bread always had to be before the Lord, in His presence. It's indicative of how the children of Israel were always before the Lord. It's also a reminder of how we are always before Him.

Bread was (is) quite necessary for life. It gives strength, and sustenance. In John's Gospel we note the following:

Jesus said,

> Verily, verily, I say unto you, except a corn of wheat fall into the ground and die, it abideth alone: but if it die, it bringeth forth much fruit (John 12:24).
>
> And he took the bread, and gave thanks, and brake it, and gave unto them, saying, This is my body which is given for you: this do in remembrance of me (Luke 22:19).

Jesus is the grain of wheat that was planted in the ground. What happens to a seed when planted in the ground? Does the ground kill the seed? Of course not; that is what gives life to it! In the same respect, Jesus was planted in the ground and came out again. Stick a seed in the ground and out will come a plant. In this case it's wheat. Jesus died and rose again. He is the living bread! We're not interested in just using all sorts of religious slogans. Those who really have been born anew can appreciate the need for the "bread of life". On a daily basis we need His bread to keep us living the authentic Christian life. We don't need the bread of life to play church. That's easy. But to walk with the Lord and really be ministers in His house, we need the strength and the sustenance that only He Himself can give--the bread of life.

> And thou shalt make a candlestick of pure gold: of beaten work shall the candlestick be made: his shaft, and his branches, his bowls, his knops, and his flowers, shall be of the same.
>
> And six branches shall come out of the sides of it; three branches of the candlestick out of the one side, and three branches of the can-

dlestick out of the other side:

Three bowls made like unto almonds, with a knop and a flower in one branch; and three bowls made like almonds in the other branch, with a knop and a flower: so in the six branches that come out of the candlestick.

And in the candlestick shall be four bowls made like unto almonds, with their knops and their flowers.

And there shall be a knop under two branches of the same, and a knop under two branches of the same, and a knop under two branches of the same, according to the six branches that proceed out of the candlestick.

Their knops and their branches shall be of the same: all it shall be one beaten work of pure gold.

And thou shalt make the seven lamps thereof: and they shall light the lamps thereof, that they may give light over against it.

And the tongs thereof, and the snuffdishes thereof, shall be of pure gold.

Of a talent of pure gold shall he make it, with all these vessels.

And look that thou make them after their pattern, which was shewed thee in the mount (Exod. 25:31-40).

The Lampstand provided light for the priests who ministered before the Lord. The Lampstand or Candlestick or Menorah is a very important symbol to the Jewish people.

Perhaps you can recall a Jewish holiday called Chanukah. This is a feast wherein we remember the eternal light in the Temple. In fact, the holiday is also called the Feast of Lights. Jesus Himself celebrated this event (see John 10:22). The light had to be burning in the Tabernacle for it was a symbol of God's presence among His people.

There was a time (167 B.C.) when the Syrians came and overtook the Temple and made it a shrine for worship of pagan deities. Finally, the Jewish people were able to take it back and reinstitute worship to Jehovah. They needed oil to burn in the Menorah, but there wasn't enough to be found. They went ahead with the limited supply that they had (only enough for one day) and God worked a miracle. The oil lasted for eight days! The light remained shining forth.

From the Temple the light went out to all the world. The brightness was a living testimony to the fact that God was shining on His people.

Jesus said that He was the real light of the world (John 8:12). How true it is! The world walks in darkness. Those who don't walk according to the light stumble over things. And so it is that those who don't follow the path shown in God's word fall into a myriad of problems, all of which could have been avoided if only they had the light! Jesus is the one who puts real light in the eyes of men and women! Here we see a picture of the light of the world--Messiah--right there in the wilderness Tabernacle.

> Moreover thou shalt make the tabernacle with ten curtains of fine twined linen, and blue, and purple, and scarlet: with cherubims of cunning work shalt thou make them.

The length of one curtain shall be eight and twenty cubits, and the breadth of one curtain four cubits: and every one of the curtains shall have one measure.

The five curtains shall be coupled together one to another; and other five curtains shall be coupled one to another.

And thou shalt make loops of blue upon the edge of the one curtain from the selvedge in the coupling; and likewise shalt thou make in the uttermost edge of another curtain, in the coupling of the second.

Fifty loops shalt thou make in the one curtain, and fifty loops shalt thou make in the edge of the curtain that is in the coupling of the second; that the loops may take hold one of another.

And thou shalt make fifty taches of gold, and couple the curtains together with the taches: and it shall be one tabernacle.

And thou shalt make curtains of goats' hair to be a covering upon the tabernacle: eleven curtains shalt thou make.

The length of one curtain shall be thirty cubits, and the breadth of one curtain four cubits: and the eleven curtains shall be all of one measure.

And thou shalt couple five curtains by themselves, and six curtains by themselves, and shalt double the sixth curtain in the forefront of the tabernacle.

And thou shalt make fifty loops on the edge of the one curtain that is outmost in the coupling, and fifty loops in the edge of the curtain which coupleth the second.

And thou shalt make fifty taches of brass, and put the taches into the loops, and couple the tent together, that it may be one.

And the remnant that remaineth of the curtains of the tent, the half curtain that remaineth, shall hang over the backside of the tabernacle.

And a cubit on the one side, and a cubit on the other side of that which remaineth in the length of the curtains of the tent, it shall hang over the sides of the tabernacle on this side and on that side, to cover it.

And thou shalt make a covering for the tent of rams' skins dyed red, and a covering above of badgers' skins.

And thou shalt make boards for the tabernacle of shittim wood standing up.

Ten cubits shall be the length of a board, and a cubit and a half shall be the breadth of one board.

Two tenons shall there be in one board, set in order one against another: thus shalt thou make for all the boards of the tabernacle.

And thou shalt make the boards for the tabernacle, twenty boards on the south side southward.

And thou shalt make forty sockets of silver under the twenty boards; two sockets under one board for his two tenons, and two sockets under another board for his two tenons.

And for the second side of the tabernacle on the north side there shall be twenty boards:

And their forty sockets of silver; two sockets under one board, and two sockets under another board.

And for the sides of the tabernacle westward thou shalt make six boards.

And two boards shalt thou make for the corners of the tabernacle in the two sides.

And they shall be coupled together beneath, and they shall be coupled together above the head of it unto one ring: thus shall it be for them both; they shall be for the two corners.

And they shall be eight boards, and their sockets of silver, sixteen sockets; two sockets under one board, and two sockets under another board.

And thou shalt make bars of shittim wood; five for the boards of the one side of the tabernacle.

> And five bars for the boards of the other side of the tabernacle, and five bars for the boards of the side of the tabernacle, for the two sides westward.
>
> And the middle bar in the midst of the boards shall reach from end to end.
>
> And thou shalt overlay the boards with gold, and make their rings of gold for places for the bars: and thou shalt overlay the bars with gold.
>
> And thou shalt rear up the tabernacle according to the fashion thereof which was shewed thee in the mount (Exod. 26:1-30).

Verses one through fourteen deal with the subject of curtains. It's no accident that the chosen fabric was linen (see verse 1). One of the fascinating aspects of Bible study is that we come to notice how the Bible is so consistent. There were many authors who contributed their hands to the task of writing Scripture. They lived in many different areas of the world (Israel, Greece, Babylon, etc.) and ministered throughout the span of many centuries. The *consistency* of their message is proof for the inspiration of the Bible. The case in point is demonstrated in the usage of linen.

God wants the Temple draped in linen. So what?

In the Book of Revelation we see a fascinating glimpse into the life of believers in the near future.

> Let us be glad and rejoice and give honour to him: for the marriage of the Lamb is come, and his wife hath made herself ready. And to her was granted that she should be arrayed in fine linen, clean and white: for the fine linen is

the righteousness of saints (Rev. 19:7,8).

The bride here is, of course, the Church--those who had responded to His proposal. What does the wife wear? Fine linen. When the time is right, the Lord comes for His bride and then she will be dressed in fine linen. Our body is the temple of the Holy Spirit and the body will be draped in linen. There is much said in Scripture about how we should keep our garments white. Let's be reminded of that now and make the connection between the Tabernacle in the wilderness and our own temples, to be someday adorned with that fine linen, clean and white.

The Tabernacle was to be dressed in fine linen and so will we. We are the temple of the Lord in a spiritual sense. It's an intriguing point and we hope that you catch the impact of it.

> And thou shalt make a veil of blue, and purple, and scarlet, and fine twined linen of cunning work: with cherubims shall it be made:
>
> And thou shalt hang it upon four pillars of shittim wood overlaid with gold: their hooks shall be of gold, upon the four sockets of silver.
>
> And thou shalt hang up the veil under the taches, that thou mayest bring in thither within the veil the ark of the testimony: and the veil shall divide unto you between the holy place and the most holy.
>
> And thou shalt put the mercy seat upon the ark of the testimony in the most holy place.

> And thou shalt set the table without the veil, and the candlestick over against the table on the side of the tabernacle toward the south: and thou shalt put the table on the north side.
>
> And thou shalt make an hanging for the door of the tent of blue, and purple, and scarlet, and fine twined linen, wrought with needle-work.
>
> And thou shalt make for the hanging five pillars of shittim wood, and overlay them with gold, and their hooks shall be of gold: and thou shalt cast five sockets of brass for them (Exod. 26:31-37).

The Veil separated the Holy of Holies from the Holy Place. The priests were not allowed to cross over into the Holy of Holies. It was an area where only the High Priest could enter. Those outside would be able to see this special curtain but never go past it. The purple and blue colors that it was made of gave a reminder of the royal nature of the Lord and the fact that He has a domain on the other side of the blue sky, heaven.

We can recall that when Messiah gave up the ghost it was reported (Matt. 27:51) that the veil in the Temple was torn in two. The Gospels make a point of this because there is something very special about that fact. The way to God has now been opened to everyone! Through the ministry of our High Priest, Jesus, we may all have direct access to the Father, and not just on the Day of Atonement, but whenever needed. The author of the Book of Hebrews tells us that we have a hope that goes behind the veil (Heb. 6:19,20).

> And thou shalt make an altar of shittim wood,

> five cubits long, and five cubits broad; the altar shall be foursquare: and the height thereof shall be three cubits.
>
> And thou shalt make the horns of it upon the four corners thereof: his horns shall be of the same: and thou shalt overlay it with brass.
>
> And thou shalt make his pans to receive his ashes, and his shovels, and his basins, and his fleshhooks, and his firepans: all the vessels thereof thou shalt make of brass.
>
> And thou shalt make for it a grate of network of brass; and upon the net shalt thou make four brasen rings in the four corners thereof.
>
> And thou shalt put it under the compass of the altar beneath, that the net may be even to the midst of the altar.
>
> And thou shalt make staves for the altar, staves of shittim wood, and overlay them with brass.
>
> And the staves shall be put into the rings, and the staves shall be upon the two sides of the altar, to bear it.
>
> Hollow with boards shalt thou make it: as it was shewed thee in the mount, so shall they make it (Exod. 27:1-8).

The brazen Altar was the place where all the animal sacrifices were brought and burned. Millions have made their way to God's altar throughout the many centuries since its creation.

We hear the psalmist exclaim:

> God is the Lord, which hath shewed us light: bind the sacrifice with cords, even unto the horns of the altar. Thou art my God, and I will praise thee: thou art my God, I will exalt thee (Psa. 118:27,28).

The event described by the psalmist was celebrated on the altar described by Moses here in Exodus. There were four horns attached to the four corners of the altar. Carcasses were tied down with ropes and then they were burned. Death for life! This is the theme of the entire Bible and it is quite essential here. In fact, *it is here where we find the basis for the Calvary of the New Testament*!

The animals had to be without any spot or blemish. Jesus was Himself without sin! The sacrifice of the offerings made atonement for sins. The death of Christ is our atonement. Actually, the ministry of Messiah is superior to this system, for here animals had to be brought frequently, but the death of Messiah was once and for all.

Not only was He the sacrifice, but He was also the High Priest. He took the sacrifice and went to the Father on behalf of those that He was doing it for. The High Priest in the Old Testament did this very thing. He would take the blood of the spotless animal and go into the Holy of Holies once a year (see Lev. 16). But Messiah went once to the Father in Heaven, taking the blood of His supreme sacrifice with Him. In so doing He made atonement once and for all!

> And thou shalt make the court of the tabernacle: for the south side southward there shall be hangings for the court of fine twined linen of an hundred cubits long for one side:

And the twenty pillars thereof and their twenty sockets shall be of brass; the hooks of the pillars and their fillets shall be of silver.

And likewise for the north side in length there shall be hangings of an hundred cubits long, and his twenty pillars and their twenty sockets of brass; the hooks of the pillars and their fillets of silver.

And for the breadth of the court on the west side shall be hangings of fifty cubits: their pillars ten, and their sockets ten.

And the breadth of the court on the east side eastward shall be fifty cubits.

The hangings of one side of the gate shall be fifteen cubits: their pillars three, and their sockets three.

And on the other side shall be hangings fifteen cubits: their pillars three, and their sockets three.

And for the gate of the court shall be an hanging of twenty cubits, of blue, and purple, and scarlet, and fine twined linen, wrought with needlework: and their pillars shall be four and their sockets four.

All the pillars round about the court shall be filleted with silver; their hooks shall be of silver, and their sockets of brass.

The length of the court shall be an hundred cubits, and the breadth fifty everywhere, and

> the height five cubits of fine twined linen, and their sockets of brass.
>
> All the vessels of the tabernacle in all the service thereof, and all the pins thereof, and all the pins of the court, shall be of brass (Exod. 27:9-19).

We had mentioned previously that the Tabernacle complex was an enclosed unit. Here now are instructions about the enclosure. We see that again fine linen was used. The entire facility was behind this linen fence. The Lord dwelt on the other side of this linen. The object of the Tabernacle was to provide a means for fellowship with the Father. In order to have that communion one had to pass through the linen.

From our previous description of the linen we learned that the linen corresponded to the righteousness of the saints. This is quite interesting because we have no righteousness of our own (see Rom. 3:10). In truth, we are made righteous through our High Priest, Jesus the Messiah.

We can't go to God's house on our own righteousness. How would we pass through the courtyard. His righteousness surrounds the place. We wouldn't make it on our own. We are given white linen garments of our own, upon receiving the Lord, when we enter through the door (John 10:9).

What is interesting to note is that the linen hangs on brass fixtures. We have already mentioned how brass corresponds to judgment. Christ has been judged for us and now our righteousness hangs on that fact.

> And thou shalt command the children of Israel, that they bring thee pure oil olive beaten for the light, to cause the lamp to burn always.

> In the tabernacle of the congregation without the veil, which is before the testimony, Aaron and his sons shall order it from evening to morning before the Lord: it shall be a statute for ever unto their generations on the behalf of the children of Israel.

We have already spoken about the Candlestick that burned in the Tabernacle and how that relates to Jesus being the light of the world. The thrust of our comments here will be related to the oil of that lamp. The oil had to be a certain specified pure oil. Jesus had the full measure of oil (see Heb. 1:9 and John 3:34). Biblically, oil corresponds to the Holy Spirit. This is illustrated in the story of Pentecost when, upon receiving the Holy Spirit, the disciples were as burning lights (see Acts 2:1-3). Jesus is the light of the world (John 8:12) and now it was time for His followers to become lights as well (Matt. 5:14). What they needed was oil and it is richly provided when a person receives the Holy Spirit of God.

The light burned in that wilderness Temple, and so now the light needs to shine through us, too, for we are the Temple of the Lord at present.

V

"The Temples Of God"

The Jerusalem Temple, frequented by the Messiah Himself, was one of the most stunning examples of ancient architecture that the human eye could behold. It was considered one of the wonders of the ancient world, and no doubt it was at the top of that list.

This was the Lord's house and one look at it would make a person like the psalmist exclaim, "I was glad when they said unto me, let us go unto the house of the Lord" (Psa. 122:1). Those who approached the Temple had the feeling that they were approaching the Lord Himself. Jesus Himself paid tribute to the Temple by giving it His divine approval (John 2:16b "My Father's house").

The Jerusalem Temple was a massive facility, a huge complex of buildings set atop Mount Moriah. This was God's house alright, but remember, at first God commanded Moses just to build Him a "mobile home" and not a permanent castle. What became this awesome shrine later on was at first a portable worship center, to be carried through a thankless wilderness by a nomad people.

The first Tabernacle was built in the year following the Exodus from Egypt. It was assembled in the middle of a desert at the foot of Mount Sinai. There were plenty of miles and plenty of years left to travel. This portable Temple was actually constructed on a detour enroute to the Promised Land. The Israelites weren't anywhere near their final destination so they needed a Tabernacle that they could efficiently pack up and take along with them.

What would have happened had the Lord not given them the Tabernacle? They would have gone on their journey and spoken about the God who visited them back at Mount Sinai. He would have been a God who manifested Himself in the past tense. Fathers would have told their young children about a God who, once upon a time in bygone days, had visited their forefathers, given some laws and then departed.

But they needed to understand that God was a God in their midst. He wasn't a deserter who just helped them out of Egypt and then left them. Rather, He was a God who was with them every step of the way, from slavery to the Promised Land! He didn't just help them; He personally led them. Granted, He didn't take the shortest route. Forty years is a long time by anyone's standards, but the delay wasn't His fault.

While enroute to the land of milk and honey, the Israelites, some two million of them, marched in an orderly fashion and set up camp in an orderly manner, as well. This was a nation on the move! People would travel with their family and the family would stay together with its tribe. The tribal leaders were given instructions about where to "park" when it was time to set up camp.

Some tribes went to the north, others to the south, some to the east and others to the west. It was the Tabernacle that was set right in the middle of the camp. It was the center-point and the tribes were instructed where to set camp with respect to where the Tabernacle tent was pitched.

The place where the people would camp was contingent upon where God would set up His camp. He wanted it clear that He was in control of things, that He was in their midst.

About three hundred and fifty years after the children of Israel arrived in the Holy Land, the Lord placed it upon the heart of the king, David, to build a home to house the Tabernacle. Up until this point the house of God remained in that aging tent! David was given the idea, but the task was to be delegated to his son, who would ascend to power after him.

Listen to the words of David's son, Solomon, the next king of Israel:

> Thou knowest how that David my father could not build an house unto the name of the Lord his God for the wars which were about him on every side, until the Lord put them under the soles of his feet.
>
> But now the Lord my God hath given me rest on every side, so that there is neither adversary nor evil occurrent.
>
> And, behold, I purpose to build an house unto the name of the Lord my God, as the Lord spake unto my father David, saying, Thy son, whom I will set upon thy throne in thy room, he shall build an house unto my name" (I Kings 5:3-5).

We read on and learn that Solomon did indeed build a Temple to the Lord, after the pattern given to Moses. Of course, this one was made with stone and other more permanent materials. Unlike the portable house, this was to be a lasting one that would stay in one place for many centuries to come. It wasn't an exact duplicate of the plan given to Moses, but the important furnishings from the wilderness Tabernacle were used in the Temple.

What did God think of this new, upgraded house? He had moved into a new neighborhood and gone from a modest dwelling to a palace. What were His thoughts?

Following the dedication ceremony which inaugurated the opening of this now completed Temple, the Lord says to Solomon:

> ...I have heard thy prayer and thy supplication, that thou hast made before me: I have

> hallowed this house, which thou hast built, to put my name there forever; and mine eyes and my heart shall be there perpetually" (I Kings 9:3).

God placed His seal of approval on this new house and everyone was quite excited. But as is often the case, we find that they grew to forget the Lord as the years passed by . Even Solomon forgot the love of his youth and went astray after other gods. Oh yes, the Temple was still there and the priests stood daily at their posts, but the flame had gone out. Not many people were interested anymore, for obedience had long since vanished.

Prophets had come and gone. The years rolled by and new men of God appeared on the scene urging the people to return to the Lord, but their messages went unheeded. Hard-heartedness was the order of the day. Judgment was promised and judgment came!

At the appointed time Judah fell to the Babylonian Empire. Those who survived were taken captive. Sadly, Judah was conquered and the Temple was finally destroyed in 586 B.C. It had stood for some four centuries, twice the age of the United States.

Jeremiah laments this tragedy in his poem known to us as the Book of Lamentations (an appropriate title), saying,

> How is the gold become dim! how is the most fine gold changed! the stones of the sanctuary are poured out in the top of every street (Lam. 4:1).

He goes on to say, as well:

> The kings of the earth, and all the inhabitants of the world, would not have believed that the adversary and the enemy should have

> entered into the gates of Jerusalem (Lam. 4:12).

Well, indeed they did enter and it wasn't just for a casual visit. They came to destroy and they did their job well! They were experts, the Babylonians, at devastation and devastate they did!

Who would have believed that the Lord would have allowed His house and His people to be crushed beneath the boots of this godless horde? Why did the Lord allow this to happen?

> For the sins of her prophets (false ones), and the iniquities of her priests (false ones, too), that have shed the blood of the just in the midst of her (Lam. 4:13).

Chastisements happen time and time again in Scripture. God isn't blind, and sin will find a person (or a nation) out. It has its consequences!

But, God gives His judgments from a Mercy Seat. Jeremiah pleads for God's favor to again shine on the Holy Land and the people that He called out of slavery to dwell therein. He prays for revival:

> Turn thou us unto thee, O Lord, and we shall be turned; renew our days as of old (Lam. 5:21).

After the period of punishment was over, the Jewish people were again allowed to return to the Promised Land. But many had become comfortable in the land of Babylon and didn't want to return to Israel. Some fifty thousand did pack up and go back to rebuild the house of the Lord (Ezra 2:1-70, esp. 64 & 65).

But then the Babylonians, who had conquered the Hebrews, were themselves overtaken in battle. The new leader, a Persian, allowed the Jews to return to their homeland. Here now is a copy of his proclamation:

> Thus saith Cyrus king of Persia, The Lord God of heaven hath given me all the kingdoms of the earth; and he hath charged me to build him an house at Jerusalem, which is in Judah.
>
> Who is there among you of all his people? his God be with him, and let him go up to Jerusalem, which is in Judah, and build the house of the Lord God of Israel, (he is the God), which is in Jerusalem" (Ezra 1:2-3).

It was now seventy years since the start of the Babylonian captivity (Jer. 29:10), and the Israelites were free to return to the land of their origin. And so they began to rebuild the house of the Lord. A few years had passed and another group came from Babylon to Jerusalem to help them restore the old theocracy. The Temple and the city were reconstructed, with difficulty, but they lacked the former glory of the previous era of Jewish civilization.

The new immigrants just didn't have the resources that Solomon had. They lacked both the money to build and the force of people to serve as builders. They did manage to reconstruct the Temple, but it wasn't nearly in the same magnitude as the first one.

A few hundred years go by and a new ruler appears on the scene by the name of Herod, known as Herod the Great. It wasn't that he was a great man; in fact there were few people in the world that had even a remote affection for him. No, he was known as the Great because he was a great builder. In order to win some kind of favor from the Jews whom he ruled (he was part Jewish himself) he made it a point to rebuild the Temple. It was this Temple that Jesus visited and some remains of it can be seen to this day. When we see pictures of the Jewish people praying at the Western Wall, it's the retaining wall of Herod's Temple that they are facing.

It was the Temple which Herod had built that was one of the wonders of the ancient world. But it wasn't just a wonder of the ancient world, it was a victim of it also. In the year 70 A.D., this celestial Jerusalem fell into a war with the Roman Empire. We have much to say about this particular destruction because the Lord Himself prophesied it and we want to draw attention to what He had to say.

The Temple constructed during the days of Herod was the one that Jesus taught in. As we said, an examination of how He responded to the Lord's house is quite fascinating and we are going to look at that very subject in the following chapter.

To wrap up our chapter on the later developments of the Tabernacle, let's remember a very salient point: the Temple was important, is important and again *will be* important in the days ahead! Why? Because contained within the confines of the Temple complex is the testimony of God's love for mankind. It's a message, a picture that tells well over a thousand words.

It's a message concerning sin, judgment and salvation, and it has been around since the most ancient of days, and it was given by a God who never changes!

VI

"There's No Place Like Home"

And when they had performed all things according to the law of the Lord, they returned into Galilee, to their own city Nazareth.

And the child grew, and waxed strong in spirit, filled with wisdom: and the grace of God was upon him.

Now his parents went to Jerusalem every year at the feast of the passover.

And when he was twelve years old, they went up to Jerusalem after the custom of the feast.

And when they had fulfilled the days, as they returned, the child Jesus tarried behind in Jerusalem; and Joseph and his mother knew not of it.

But they, supposing him to have been in the company, went a day's journey; and they sought him among their kinsfolk and acquaintance.

And when they found him not, they turned back again to Jerusalem, seeking him.

And it came to pass, that after three days they found him in the temple, sitting in the midst of

> the doctors, both hearing them, and asking them questions.
>
> And all that heard him were astonished at his understanding and answers.
>
> And when they saw him, they were amazed: and his mother said unto him, Son, why hast thou thus dealt with us? behold, thy father and I have sought thee sorrowing.
>
> And he said unto them, How is it that ye sought me? wist ye not that I must be about my Father's business?
>
> And they understood not the saying which he spake unto them.
>
> And he went down with them, and came to Nazareth, and was subject unto them: but his mother kept all these sayings in her heart.
>
> And Jesus increased in wisdom and stature, and in favour with God and man (Luke 2:39-52).

Luke has been called the "royal photographer" of the New Testament, and with good reason. It was he, more than the others, who took us behind the scenes to get a more personal glimpse of the early boyhood of Jesus. In his Gospel we can see what was perhaps Messiah's first experience in the house that God built. It was in that house, at the age of twelve, that Jesus first announced, "...I must be about my Father's business..." (Luke 2:49).

Of course, it's difficult to imagine what was in the mind of our Lord when He visited the Temple as a youngster, or while conversing with the sages of Israel there. Yet, we can safely assume that He felt strong stirrings within as He visited His Father's house.

Dorothy, in the film classic "The Wizard of Oz," is seen clicking her heels together saying, "There's no place like home, there's no place like home." Some question the underlying theme of this fable, but no one calls into question the sentiment of a young child's longing for that good old home-sweet-home.

Have you ever gone back to pay a visit to the old house where you were raised? There's something that happens to us when we visit the place where we grew up. The visit brings back memories and sometimes we can almost visualize the family together. It can bring up a surge of emotions as we reflect upon the bygone days of yesteryear.

There was just something about that old house and it served to bring out the strongest of passions in Jesus (see John 2:12-17).

When did Jesus realize who He was? Granted, it sounds like a silly question, but think about it. When Jesus was there in His playpen, as a very young child, did He know who He really was? Was He saying to Himself, "Here I am God in the flesh?" We all know how babies tend to act like gods! Face it, they constantly demand our affection, attention and adoration. But what about this very special child? Did He know who He was at that very tender age?

We really have no way of knowing for sure, but we can glean from the Scriptures insights into the very first time that He articulated an awareness of His special relationship to the Father. As Jewish boys approach their thirteenth year, they become what's called "Bar-Mitzvah" (son of the commandment). This is the moment when they assume full citizenship in the religious community of Israel. They become men, so to speak. It was during this season in His earthly life that Messiah first articulated "...I must be about *My Father's* business...."

Could it have been that it all came together in the mind of the young Jesus when He made that visit to the house of the Lord? It was as though something moved deep within His soul. Furthermore, what was God's business in that house? It was all about sacrifice for sins, death for life. Was it here that Jesus realized His full calling?

The Temple was the object of all Israel's affection, but our modern humane society would have closed the place down, for this was the site of much slaughter. Jewish historians tell us that as many as three hundred thousand lambs were slain every day just during the Passover season alone!

The story in Luke's Gospel takes place during the Passover holiday. No doubt the young Jesus could hear the bleating of the many thousands of sheep being taken off to the slaughter. The smoke of the sacrificial lambs would ascend toward the heavens and Jesus would have breathed in the stench of it all.

It was the smell of death, but it was death that brought life. Jesus articulated His awareness of His unique calling there during this season. "I must be about My Father's business." Approximately twenty-one years later, during another Passover season, Jesus looked up and said, "It is finished" (John 19:30). He understood His Father's business very well and at Calvary the work was done; His "business trip" was over.

It all started with a trip to the Temple and it ended that way, as well. What's in a house? Well, there is obviously something to be said about this one. The Temple did something to Jesus. The remains of it are still here to this day. Perhaps you should visit the site yourself and see what kind of impression it leaves on you.

It is quite clear that Jesus felt strongly about the house of His Father. This manor was God's mysterious message to the world. Jesus understood what it was saying; in fact He *was* what it was saying. It's all in the house, friends!

Having traced the developments of the Lord's house

from Moses to Jesus, we'll now proceed to look ahead. The Temple of the past makes for an interesting study, but so does the Temple of the future!

Will there be a future Temple in the coming days?

VII

"I Am God!"

Many Christians are puzzled about the subject of end-times events. Why? Quite simply, it's because Bible prophecy is like a puzzle. We've all worked puzzles at one time or another. Let's think back to what they were like.

You opened the box and found an assortment of shapes, sizes and colors. After dumping them on the table, you began the process of sorting them all out and putting them all together. It took a lot of patience on your part. What propelled you to press on through this painstaking process? You determined in your mind that you wanted to see the completed picture and you derived personal satisfaction as you strove toward that objective.

The same principle holds true for biblical interpretation. In particular, end-times prophecy is like a puzzle with a very large assortment of pieces. There's a lot of work to be done and it's easy to get frustrated as we sort through the box seeking to connect the pieces one to another. How's your picture coming?

Let's see now: There's a Rapture over here and a Tribulation Temple over there. There's a false christ over there and a Second Coming of the real Christ over here. What comes first? What follows what? What goes where?

Can we get some help in putting all of this together?

It's a frustrating task to begin with and to make matters even more perplexing, we are warned about the false teachers that will appear on the scene to lead many astray (Matt. 24:5). People do not generally understand Bible prophecy and are increasingly wary of those who claim that they do. Question: Is there a way out of this quagmire? Is there really a way to put this particularly important puzzle together?

Do you find yourself baffled as you wrestle with the intricate equations of end-times scenarios? If so, then you need to better acquaint yourself with the basics. After all, if you don't have addition and subtraction down pat, how can you expect to succeed at handling more advanced mathematics? By the same token, if you aren't familiar with the basic themes of Bible prophecy, you will easily get lost in the puzzle that you so much want to put together!

Where does one go to get the basics of end-time prophecy? Must we all go to a renowned Bible college or seminary? Of course not! Where then? A trip to our local Bible is a great place to start (and finish).

Jesus said, "Ye call me Master and Lord: and ye say well; for so I am" (John 13:13). He's the teacher! It's important to acquaint ourselves with what He said.

In the 24th chapter of the Gospel of Matthew we find one of the Scripture's most comprehensive surveys of end-time events. Jesus Himself is teaching here on a wide range of matters pertaining to the last days. We could write a dozen books on this chapter alone, but for our purposes here, we'll confine ourselves to the chapter's introduction, along with that which pertains to the Tribulation Temple.

To begin with, let's reacquaint ourselves with the Lord's own words:

> And Jesus went out, and departed from the temple: and his disciples came to him for to shew him the buildings of the temple. And Jesus said unto them, See ye not all these things? verily I say unto you, there shall not be left here one stone upon another that shall not be thrown down (Matt. 24:1,2).

It was just two days before the King would wear His crown on the Calvary cross. Knowing full well that His earthly ministry was about to draw to a close, Jesus paid a final and dangerous visit to this Temple in Jerusalem. As He was departing, He was met by a band of His disciples who were totally enthralled by the Temple complex. However, their ecstasy was short-lived, for they were informed that the house of God, which they so adored, would soon be utterly destroyed!

They had great hopes, but this particular Temple was not to be the palace of the messianic Kingdom.

With Messiah's prediction of doom fresh in their minds, they proceeded to ask Him:

> ...Tell us, when shall these things be? and what shall be the sign of thy coming, and of the end of the world? (Matt. 24:3)

The Olivet discourse, His response to their inquiries, has held readers spellbound for the last 2,000 years:

> And Jesus answered and said unto them, Take heed that no man deceive you. For many shall come in my name, saying, I am Christ; and shall deceive many. And ye shall hear of wars and rumours of wars: see that ye be not troubled: for all these things must come to pass, but the end is not yet. For nation shall rise against nation, and kingdom against kingdom: and there shall be famines, and pestilences, and earthquakes, in divers places. All these are the beginning of sorrows.
>
> Then shall they deliver you up to be afflicted, and shall kill you: and ye shall be hated of all nations for my name's sake. And then shall

> many be offended, and shall betray one another, and shall hate one another. And many false prophets shall rise, and shall deceive many. And because iniquity shall abound, the love of many shall wax cold. But he that shall endure unto the end, the same shall be saved. And this gospel of the kingdom shall be preached in all the world for a witness unto all nations; and then shall the end come" (Matt. 24:4-14).

The chapter opened with Messiah predicting that the Temple would be destroyed. He then went on to describe the period commonly known as the "Tribulation". Following these disastrous predictions, Jesus gave a clue to one of the period's most important developments, an event which has significance that cannot be overstated!

> When ye therefore shall see the abomination of desolation, spoken of by Daniel the prophet, stand in the holy place (whoso readeth, let him understand) (Matt. 24:15).

Let's back up for a minute in order to get an overview of the entire chapter. Jesus began by predicting the devastation of the Jerusalem Temple. History moves under the omnipotent hand of God, and in the year 70 A.D., Titus, the Roman general, destroyed the Jerusalem Temple. The ruins of that debacle can be seen to this day, for the Temple has not been rebuilt since then. But in verse 15, Jesus speaks of a terrible desecration that will take place in the "holy place" during the future Tribulation Period.

The Apostle Paul gives us further confirmation of this event, saying:

> ...that man of sin (antichrist) be revealed...Who opposeth and exalteth himself

> above all that is called God, or that is worshipped; so that he as God sitteth in the temple of God, shewing himself that he is God (II Thess. 2:3b-4).

Paul reminds the church at Thessalonica that one day the Antichrist will enter the Temple of God and proclaim that he is God! In order for him to do this, there will need to be a proper Temple of God there in Jerusalem. The Temple will one day be rebuilt and the Antichrist will snatch it away claiming that he is God and that the Temple really belongs to him!

History leaves us with many examples of people who strode about declaring that they were the returned Christ. Claiming godship has been around since the days of antiquity. What is interesting to note about this "god" is that he is able to pull it off! The world will take him very seriously. He will amass the power to overthrow all other forms of worldly religion and establish himself at the head of a one-world religious system that will have its headquarters in the Temple of Jerusalem!

The Apostle John adds insights on this very event, commenting on how the world will be seduced by this fiend. John observes:

> ...all the world wondered after the beast...and they worshipped the beast, saying, Who is like unto the beast? (Rev. 13:3b-4)

There is much to be said about all of this. Here we want to again state the obvious. First: During the Tribulation Period there is a rebuilt Temple. Second: The Antichrist ascends to power and is able to violate this Temple, proclaiming that he is God incarnate.

If one follows the path of concrete observations, he is led to concrete conclusions. Through our brief exegesis of the previous passages, we may deduce the following: The

Temple, the focal point of Old Testament worship, plays an integral part in the unfolding drama of the New Testament.

If you're looking for valuable pieces to your end time puzzle, then be sure to keep that vital point in mind.

One of the fascinating aspects of biblical hermeneutics is that every time you get an answer to one question you find that your conclusion gives birth to a myriad of other questions. In this case, who is going to build the Temple? What will be the design? Where will it be rebuilt? When will it be constructed? And, why hasn't it been rebuilt already?

These questions are answered in depth in the definitive book, Satan in the Sanctuary (by Zola Levitt and Dr. Thomas McCall, Moody Press, updated 1987, available through this ministry). Suffice it here to say that the Jewish people, who badly want to rebuild the Temple, will do so at such a time as they are able. And that means as soon as the site is clear!

The notion of a rebuilt Temple has been in the Jewish prayerbooks for millenia. The mere thought of this dramatic milestone happening ignites a flame of passion that burns deep within the heart of Judaism's orthodox communities. One can visit the Western Wall (the remains of the old Temple) on any day of the year, at any time of day, and find devout Jews praying that the holy place will again be rebuilt. And they aren't just praying. Some say that plans have been drawn up and young Jewish men from the tribe of Levi are preparing to be priests in a rebuilt sanctuary!

When one goes to the Western Wall to witness Jewish people praying there, he also sees a golden dome looming overhead, casting down its shadow from the other side of the Wall. There stands one of the most sacred religious sites of the Islamic world--the Mosque of Omar. Two objects cannot occupy the same space at the same time. So, before the Temple goes up, that mosque must come down!

Were Israel to even suggest a date for reconstruction, an alarm would sound forth throughout the entire Moslem world, calling for an all-out "Holy War" against the Jews. At present Israel certainly does not have the means to hold off such an extensive fanatical uprising.

But, in the not-too-distant future, the Antichrist will evidently demonstrate an ability to "stay the hand" of the Moslem hordes, thus allowing for Temple reconstruction.

He will make a covenant with Israel at the beginning of the Tribulation Period, possibly containing a clause stipulating that a reconstructed Jewish Temple will be part of their terms of endearment.

In a short time, the Antichrist's uncanny acumen will catapult him to world renown. He not only will seem to solve the Mid-East dilemma, but he'll also bring about a cessation of global hostility, creating an impression that the long awaited messianic era has arrived. It will look like the peaceful messianic era and will sound like it as well. For that matter, it'll even "taste" like it, as mankind for a season will be satiated by the fruits of a conjured-up prosperity.

Prior to the advent of the Antichrist, the true Church will have been Raptured from a world staggering beneath the burdens imposed by its harsh taskmaster -- the evil one himself. Darkness will have covered the earth, as today's problems escalate to proportions never before experienced since the dawn of creation.

And then, from a distant horizon, an angel of light shall arise bringing healing on his wings. They'll think he's the Savior, not realizing that beneath his soothing exterior lurks a serpent, who only intends to kill his prey before he eats it!

He'll swoop down on a deluded world, and beneath their failing eyes he'll build his snake den behind the ramparts of the Tribulation Temple!

VIII

"Moving Back To The Old Neighborhood"

The Great Tribulation will draw to a close with this rabid vulture mustering his brood together to do battle with the Lord when He returns. The Raptured Church had previously ascended to meet the Lord in the air (I Thess. 4:16,17). Now, with the intent of thwarting a successful return of Christ to rule, the Prince of Darkness will lead his troops to meet the Lord on the ground. What will ensue shall be the world's all-time most dreaded conflict--the battle of Armageddon! John reports:

> And I saw three unclean spirits like frogs come out of the mouth of the dragon, and out of the mouth of the beast, and out of the mouth of the false prophet.
>
> For they are the spirits of devils, working miracles, which go forth unto the kings of the earth and of the whole world, to gather them to the battle of that great day of God Almighty (Rev. 16 :13,14).

With the black chess pieces in place, it's time now to examine the position that develops on the other side of the board. John goes on to exclaim:

> And I saw heaven opened, and behold a white horse; and he that sat upon him was called Faithful and True, and in righteousness he doth judge and make war.

His eyes were as a flame of fire, and on his head were many crowns; and he had a name written, that no man knew, but he himself.

And He was clothed with a vesture dipped in blood: and his name is called The Word of God.

And the armies which were in heaven followed him upon white horses, clothed in fine linen, white and clean.

And out of his mouth goeth a sharp sword, that with it he should smite the nations: and he shall rule them with a rod of iron: and he treadeth the winepress of the fierceness and wrath of Almighty God.

And he hath on his vesture and on his thigh a name written, KING OF KINGS, AND LORD OF LORDS.

And I saw an angel standing in the sun; and he cried with a loud voice, saying to all the fowls that fly in the midst of heaven, Come and gather yourselves together unto the supper of the great God;

That ye may eat the flesh of kings, and the flesh of captains, and the flesh of mighty men, and the flesh of horses, and of them that sit on them, and the flesh of all men, both free and bond, both small and great.

And I saw the beast, and the kings of the earth, and their armies, gathered together to make war against him that sat on the horse, and against his army (Rev. 19:11-19).

What transpires when the Prince of Darkness squares off against the King of Light? Checkmate in one move! John continues:

> And the beast was taken, and with him the false prophet that wrought miracles before him, with which he deceived them that had received the mark of the beast, and them that worshipped his image. These both were cast alive into a lake of fire burning with brimstone.
>
> And the remnant were slain with the sword of him that sat upon the horse, which sword proceeded out of his mouth: and all the fowls were filled with their flesh.
>
> And I saw an angel come down from heaven, having the key of the bottomless pit and a great chain in his hand.
>
> And he laid hold on the dragon, that old serpent, which is the Devil, and Satan, and bound him a thousand years,
>
> And cast him into the bottomless pit, and shut him up, and set a seal upon him, that he should deceive the nations no more, till the thousand years should be fulfilled: and after that he must be loosed a little season (Rev. 19:20-20:3).

The match is now over and the black pieces are swept off the board. From this point on, the believers need no longer beseech God with the words of the Lord's Prayer,

"Our Father which art in heaven...thy kingdom come: Thy will be done..." Why not? Because He is no longer a Father in heaven for He has arrived on earth, His Kingdom has come and His will is done! John's words speak of His glorious arrival!

The binding and casting away of the devil will inaugurate the period known as the Millennium. The word "millennium" is Latin for "a thousand years".

'Tis the real season to be jolly! Listen to the jubilant exaltations of the Old Testament prophets, as they foresaw this magnificent event, and what would follow as a result of it:

ZECHARIAH
(written 520-518 BC)

> And the Lord shall be king over all the earth: in that day shall there be one Lord, and his name one (Zech. 14:9).

DANIEL
(written 537 BC)

> And there was given him dominion, and glory, and a kingdom, that all people, nations, and languages, should serve him: his dominion is an everlasting dominion, which shall not pass away, and his kingdom that which shall not be destroyed (Dan. 7:14).

ISAIAH
(written 740-680 BC)

> And many people shall go and say, Come ye, and let us go up to the mountain of the Lord, to *the house of the God of Jacob*; and he will teach us of his ways, and we will walk in his

> paths: for out of Zion will go forth the law, and the word of the Lord from Jerusalem (Isa. 2:3).

What? Did you hear that? There's that Temple again! Question: What does the Lord's house on top of God's mountain sound like to you? Question: The law will proceed from where? Is it Washington, D. C. that the word ushers forth from? Is it Rome? How about Mecca? No, it's Jerusalem, the city of the great King!

The reason why we are drawing your attention to a lot of Bible passages is because we don't want you to think that we just have some biased philosophy. When we talk about this subject, some folks will undoubtedly say, "You fellows have interesting perspectives." This is not the sort of thing that we are interested in conveying; rather, we want it to be perfectly clear: God's future plans for Jerusalem's exaltation and the like are rooted in *His very own words* and not in our minds. Scripture says what it means and it means what it says!

Hear now the very words of the prophet Isaiah, as he further illuminates the subject of the millennial era:

> Of the increase of his government and peace there shall be no end, upon the throne of David, and upon his kingdom, to order it, and to establish it with judgment and with justice from henceforth even for ever... (Isa. 9:7).

In order to administer justice and government, one needs a location to administer from, and the "White House" of the messianic era will be that grand old Jerusalem Temple of God. Dignitaries from foreign lands come to America now and meet with our head of state on "Capitol Hill". Likewise, during the Millennial reign of Christ on earth, the nations of the world will come and pay their respects to Him. Take notice of the words of the prophet Zechariah:

> And it shall come to pass, that everyone that is left of all the nations which came against Jerusalem shall even go up from year to year to worship the King, the Lord of hosts... (Zech. 14:16).

He even went on to describe a punishment for those who would not go to worship the Lord in Jerusalem.

> And it shall be, that whoso will not come up of all the families of the earth unto Jerusalem to worship the King, the Lord of hosts, even upon them shall be no rain (Zech. 14:17).

We hope by now that the idea of a future exaltation of Israel, the Holy Land, is firmly fixed in your mind. This isn't just the fanciful dreamings of two Jewish authors, and the selections of verses given (and there are many more) should attest to that fact more than adequately. The reason we wish to belabor this point is that there are those who tend to take the promises of the Bible and create their own applications, devoid of the original intentions of the passages. This simply isn't a legitimate way to "divide the word of truth".

Let's now turn our attention to the meat of this study. All of this so far has been the appetizer. The main course will be found in the book of Ezekiel, where the prophet gave us a graphic portrait of life in the Millennial Kingdom. The prophet of God bequeathed to us exhaustive instructions regarding the messianic "White House," along with detailing some of what will transpire therein. At this juncture it would be a good idea for you to put this book down and read the closing chapters of the book of Ezekiel (chapters 40 to 48). Afterwards, join us again, and we'll exegete the text to hopefully make it a little easier for you to understand certain relevant parts of it.

****

Ezekiel spent his developing years being bathed in the rays of light shining forth from the Jerusalem Temple. Born into a priestly family, he was destined to become a minister in the courts of the Lord--the holy Temple. His career was cut short before it ever really got off the ground, for the young Ezekiel was torn away from the city and Temple he loved, and carried off in the deportation by Nebuchadnezzar (586 B.C.), to spend the remainder of his life in Babylonian exile.

Like his contemporary Daniel, Ezekiel likewise saw the "handwriting on the wall". He was well aware of the sins of his estranged countrymen. He was outside of the Holy Land, but they were outside of the will of God, and it was only a question of time until their sins would find them out. From Babylon, Ezekiel the prophesier foretold the terrible fate that would befall the Jews in Israel. In the first half of his book, chapters 1-24, he warns about the catastrophic end that will result in their death or exile, and the razing of the Temple. When the city was finally sacked, Ezekiel changed the tone of his messages to one of hope and conciliation for the people of God. He preached good news about a coming new Jerusalem that would one day rise up upon the ruins of the then (and now) decimated holy city. Listen to his words of comfort to the exiled Jews in Babylon following the fall of the Temple:

> And David my servant shall be king over them (David had been dead for many hundreds of years at this juncture); and they all shall have one shepherd: they shall also walk in my judgments, and observe my

> statutes, and do them.
>
> And they shall dwell in the land that I have given unto Jacob my servant, wherein your fathers have dwelt; and they shall dwell therein, even they, and their children, and their children's children for ever: and my servant David shall be their prince forever.
>
> Moreover I will make a covenant of peace with them; it shall be an everlasting covenant with them: and I will place them, and multiply them, and will set my sanctuary in the midst of them for evermore.
>
> My tabernacle also shall be with them: yea, I will be their God, and they shall be my people.
>
> And the heathen shall know that I the Lord do sanctify Israel, when my sanctuary shall be in the midst of them for evermore" (Ezek. 37:24-28).

Here we notice how Ezekiel is binding up the broken-hearted. He is preaching good news to the captives. He's wiping away the tears from their eyes by encouraging them that one day the Lord will build a Temple that never will be destroyed! He goes on to speak of a day when the King of Kings will return again to take His seat among His people and inhabit the dwelling place that He had constructed for Himself.

Ezekiel left exact instructions about the future house of God. Let's concern ourselves with the particulars of this future regal estate--the Millennial Temple.

The exhaustive blueprints found in 40:1-43:27 are not easy to understand at first reading, but the rendering of an image to work with certainly is not impossible. His description of the future Temple begins with measurements of the outer court and outer gates (40:5-27). From there he proceeds to describe the inner courts and gates (40:28-47) and then the Temple proper (40:48-41:26).

There are those who claim that the Temple spoken of by Ezekiel was the one that was rebuilt when the Jews returned from the 70-year exile in Babylon (see Jer. 25:12 and Ezra 1:1-4). Having said that, they go on to assert that the idea of a rebuilt Temple is not in God's plan and that the verses which seem to indicate to the contrary were simply predictions of the Temple that Ezra came back to rebuild. They claim that there are no longer any predictions about a coming literal Temple.

This objection is rather simple to deal with. First of all, the Temple built by the exiles who returned from captivity was not even comparable to Solomon's original, let alone the one predicted by Ezekiel. The prophet Haggai laments that the diminutive accomplishment of the returned Temple builders was nothing in comparison to Solomon's Temple (Hag. 2:3). And secondly, the Temple spoken of by Ezekiel will never be destroyed (Ezek. 37:26-28). Obviously, the previously built Temples are long since gone.

Following his description of the Temple's architectural design, Ezekiel goes on to describe the Lord's return to the Temple.

> Afterward he brought me to the gate, even the gate that looketh toward the east:
>
> And, behold, the glory of the God of Israel came from the way of the east: and his voice was like a noise of many waters: and the earth shined with his glory.
>
> And the glory of the Lord came into the

> house by the way of the gate whose prospect is toward the east.
>
> So the spirit took me up, and brought me into the inner court; and, behold, the glory of the Lord filled the house (Ezek. 43:1-5).

Ezekiel had a lot to say about the subject of the Lord's literal return, but he didn't have a monopoly on this very important area of biblical eschatology. Other prophets comment on the triumphal re-entry of the Lord into His dwelling place on earth.

> ...I am returned unto Zion, and will dwell in the midst of Jerusalem: and Jerusalem shall be called a city of truth; and the mountain of the Lord of hosts the holy mountain (Zech. 8:3).

The Old Testament draws to a close with the following promise uttered from the mouth of Malachi:

> ...and the Lord, whom ye seek, shall suddenly come to his temple, even the messenger of the covenant, whom ye delight in: behold, he shall come... (Mal. 3:1).

Fasten your seatbelts friends, you are about to enter into an area of controversy.

It is a point of controversy that when the Lord returns to His Temple, He will again institute the Old Testament sacrificial system. It is quite clear that offerings, thought to be finished at the cross, will again be used in the service of worshipping God. But don't take our word for it; rather, pay close attention to the following words spoken by God to Ezekiel:

> And he said unto me, Son of man, thus saith the Lord God; These are the ordinances of the altar in the day when they shall make it, to offer burnt offerings thereon, and to sprinkle blood thereon (Ezek. 43:18).

You may be saying to yourself, "Now wait one minute here! I can appreciate this Jewish perspective that the Hebrew Christians offer, but I cannot believe that one day I will be returning to the law. Because Paul said, 'For Christ is the end of the law for righteousness to everyone that believeth..." (Rom. 10:4).

In this case, it really looks like you have Ezekiel in one corner and Paul in the other. It seems that a contradiction exists between those two. Before clearing up that problem, we want to make matters even worse-looking!

Paul said that Christ was the "end of the law". But let's examine something Paul did when he came to Jerusalem after preaching to the non-Jews.

> Then Paul took the men, and the next day *purifying himself* with them (Levitical worship) *entered into the temple*, to signify the accomplishment of the days of purification, *until that an offering should be offered for every one of them* (Acts 21:26).

It is clear from the New Testament that Paul the Apostle visited the Temple and made sacrifices, etc. Was he a hypocrite, saying one thing and doing something else? We don't think so. He wasn't the only apostle that worshipped God in the Temple after the day of Pentecost. Let's look at some of the others:

> *Now Peter and John went up together into the temple* at the hour of prayer, being the ninth hour (Acts 3:1).

Notice what the New Testament reveals about the first church in general:

> And they, continuing daily with one accord *in the temple*, and breaking bread from house to house, did eat their meat with gladness and singleness of heart,
>
> Praising God, and having favour with all the people. And the Lord added to the church daily such as should be saved (Acts 2:46, 47).

This may startle many, and a thousand objections may be raised, but the truth of the matter is that the first church lived and functioned as Jews. Granted, they were Jewish believers in Messiah Jesus, but being such did not in their minds imply a break with the ancestral religion. They didn't see a throwing away of the law as part of their Christian duty. Why not? Because they understood how the Messiah was represented by the Law. They understood the meaning of these various sacrifices as being memorials to Messiah who was the real sin offering, once and for all.

The Church has the "Lord's Supper" as a memorial to celebrate the death of Messiah until He returns. Paul says, "For as often as ye eat this bread, and drink the cup, ye do shew the Lord's death *till he come*" (I Cor. 11:26). When He comes, we will no longer celebrate that which was instituted only until He comes; rather, we (restored Israel and the Church) will celebrate the Old Testament memorial--the Lamb of God in the altar.

The Levitical system looked forward to the coming of the Messiah. Israel as a nation didn't respond to Jesus, and because the King was rejected (by the nation as a whole) there was no chance at that time for the Kingdom. The Kingdom was taken away from them for the time being (see Matt. 21:43) and a new organism was born shortly thereafter--the Church.

There will be a time, in the not-too-distant future, when Israel (as a nation) will respond to the Messiah Jesus. Hear what Zechariah said:

> And I will pour upon the house of David, and upon the inhabitants of Jerusalem, the spirit of grace and of supplications: and they shall look upon me whom they have pierced, and they shall mourn for him, as one mourneth for his only son... (Zech. 12:10).

When Jesus returns to establish the Kingdom, Israel, at that time, will respond and be joined with the Church, and both together will serve the King of Israel. At that time the law will again be instituted in light of its real meaning: the death, burial and resurrection of Messiah. (For more information on how the law relates to Jesus, see The Seven Feasts of Israel, available through this ministry.)

Paul's usage of the expression, "end of the law" is in the context of one trying to establish righteousness by means of it. This is impossible, (see Heb. 10:4). Messiah is the "end of the law *for righteousness*". Only belief in Jesus Christ can make a person righteous.

What then is the purpose of the law? Simply, it's there to point the way to Messiah. In ancient days the law pointed *forward* to Jesus. In the Millennial era, the law will be used to point *back* to Him. The word "end" that Paul used, is the Greek word *telos*, which in this case has to do with a "purpose or goal". In other words, it all points to Jesus and has its termination in Him.

The law must be understood in light of its fulfillment, and in the Millennial era it will be celebrated in the light of His presence (Ezek. 43:18-27). It is clear from the Scriptures that there will be a Temple in the Millennium and that sacrifice will be part of the ritual there, as it has always been.

Having established these two important points, we now turn our attention to the fact that old holy days of ancient Israel will be celebrated in the Kingdom as well.

> In the first month, in the fourteenth day of the month, ye shall have the *passover*, a feast of seven days; unleavened bread shall be eaten.
>
> And upon that day shall the prince prepare for himself and for all the people of the land a bullock for a sin offering.
>
> And seven days of the feast he shall prepare a burnt-offering to the Lord, seven bullocks and seven rams without blemish daily the seven days; and a kid of the goats daily for a sin-offering.
>
> And he shall prepare a meat-offering of an ephah for a bullock, and an ephah for a ram, and an hin of oil for an ephah.
>
> In the seventh month, in the fifteenth day of the month (this is the Jewish feast called *Tabernacles*), shall he do the like in the feast of the seven days, according to the sin-offering, and according to the burnt-offering, and according to the meat offering, and according to the oil" (Ezek. 45:21-25).

We conclude this chapter in the hope that we have stimulated your thinking. There is a lot to be learned about the Millennial era and the Temple that will be revitalized during that time. Temple worship, like that of ancient times in "the house that God built," will be part of the lives of all

Christians for a thousand years in the Kingdom to come.

Conclusion

It's our sincere desire that you acquire a feeling of urgency regarding the Lord's imminent return. Not only do we want you to grasp these impending events for yourself, but we want you to encourage others in this regard, "...as you see the day drawing near" (Heb. 10:25).

The Lord's house described in this book will become God's Kingdom "White House". During the infamous Tribulation Period, the Antichrist will seize control of the Temple, using it as a headquarters for his one-world religion. His diabolical plan will be thwarted when He is defeated by the Lord in the battle of Armageddon, when the King comes in His glory. Then the real Messianic Palace will be built and inhabited by the Messiah of Israel, who will rule from there throughout the Millenial era. This final Temple, the Millenial Temple, is described in Ezekiel 40-48.

There is much to be said about all of this. Exhaustive works have been written, by scholars more able than ourselves, on the events which precede the coming of the Lord. We have done little more than introduce you to a rather complicated field of study. We hope that you have been able to glean some important insights from our brief sketch. We wanted to communicate these things to you in a manner that was pleasant, easy to read, informative and inspirational. If we have been able to do this, then we have reached our objective.

For further studies into Bible prophecy and related subjects, we'd suggest that you contact our ministry about our Institute of Jewish and Christian Studies. We have developed an entire systematic program for the more serious Bible students. It may very well be that you would benefit from a more detailed approach. In addition, we have a growing library of books related to biblical prophecy. Contact our office and we'd be happy to send you a newsletter with a booklist.

And, as we always remind you, *Sha'alu shalom Yerushalayim* -- "Pray for the peace of Jerusalem."